STYLIST

THE INTERPRETERS OF FASHION

FOREWORD BY ANNA WINTOUR
TEXT BY SARAH MOWER
CREATIVE DIRECTION BY RAUL MARTINEZ

STYLE.COM IN ASSOCIATION WITH *Rizzoli* NEW YORK

FOREWORD

Although I was for years a fashion sittings editor, I was never particularly good at it. Which is not to say that I was untalented, but that I was always conscious that there existed, high in the stratosphere, stylists whose gifts I simply did not have. What are these gifts? What is it that makes one picture of a dress seem humdrum and another legendary? Once, in an attempt to explore this question, I commissioned five stylists to photograph the same off-white Calvin Klein skirt-suit. It was the mid-eighties, and I was working at *New York* magazine. One—Tonne Goodman, who appears in this book—sent back an image that was simple, chic, and very "Katharine Hepburn." Another created a wedding scene. A third gave me a forties diva with a big hat, lots of jewels, lots of dogs. A fourth—who I happily work with to this day—never returned my call. A fifth sent in a Robert Mapplethorpe image of a bald man wearing just the jacket.

However, I still don't exactly know how to account for the visual imagination of the people in this book. It's clear from their biographies that you cannot be taught how to be a great fashion editor, indeed cannot hope to achieve it at some point in the future. Either you've got it or you haven't; and if you've got it, you've had it from a very early age. With luck, you'll meet a photographer with a shared sensibility, and you'll immediately begin to produce images that stand out from the rest. The role of the camera is crucial. It's not a coincidence that so many of these artists have worked extensively with Richard Avedon, Steven Meisel, Steven Klein, Arthur Elgort, Patrick Demarchelier, and Juergen Teller. I wish that I could break down the chemistry between the collaborators. I can only suggest that it remains as elusive, and as powerful, as the chemistry of a good marriage.

One thing that struck me, in reading this book, is the degree to which the fashion editor's visual perspective is governed by his or her earliest years. The gardens, the schools, the neighbors, the light—all are signifiers that come back again and again in the work of the grown child. So although fashion is completely implicated in the transitory—clothes are here today, gone tomorrow—and stylists are by professional inclination the first to seek out change and trends, beneath the froth, in a great stylist, is a deep pool of memory and longing. It's down there that the extraordinary images swim from.

ANNA WINTOUR

V

INTRODUCTION

Since the turn of the millennium, the term "stylist" has shot from obscurity to everyday pop-usage without, so far, being pinned down precisely in any dictionary. It's easy to see why: on the one hand, its meaning has been moving so rapidly, but on the other, it seems to apply to such diffuse, mysterious, behind-the-scenes skills that only the innermost inhabitants of the fashion world can fully understand what they are. In recent times, the tabloid press has shrunk the term to a synonym for people paid to dress celebrities—people who now often vie with their clients for recognition.

However visible, though, that brand of stylist is only a narrow subsection of a largely uncharted profession whose talents are much wider, more nuanced, and far-reaching. Within it is an elite: individuals whose supercharged sensitivity to the visual—and sometimes their cutting wit—helps formulate the background aesthetics of every decade. They are the coauthors of some of the most powerful imagery that hits us every time we flip open a magazine, glimpse a fashion show, flick on a TV or computer, or drive past a billboard. Yet still they remain mysterious.

These are the editors, image-makers, taste-formers, and visual provocateurs who are the subject of this book. At the most basic level, their job can be described as putting the clothes in the picture. That task—of selecting and documenting clothes—can sound humble (and often is, as everyone who has ever been a fashion assistant can attest), but what binds the diverse talents in these pages together is the ability to make the clothes part of a bigger story. The best of their work has the power to transcend fashion trends, and to reflect something symbolic, joyful or, on occasion, chilling about the times we live in.

The ability to put x with y in an original way; to pick out one quintessential detail for scrutiny on a page; or to treat clothes as costume for a flight of narrative, cinematic fantasy—all these lie within the spectrum of talents of great stylists. Their influence works on many levels. Brilliant styling can sell clothes, change the way we want to dress, propose revolutionary ideas about who and what is beautiful, inform fantasies about where and how we'd like to live. It discovers new models, promotes the talent of new designers, and inspires established ones to see their clothes in a new light. In the endless relay race of fashion, great stylists are the ones who pass on the baton for the season to come, reinterpreting what they've seen on the runway to predict what will happen next.

Through the fashion marketing boom of the 1980s and the explosive changes in global communication of the '90s and the new millennium, designers and executives in cosmetics, music, and advertising have come to value and rely upon these talents. The work of influential stylists has spun off into new media (like the music video), crossed over into neighboring genres (such as fine art photography), and participated in the higher echelons of celebrity image-making. Anyone who needs to find a universally intelligible visual language in order to sell to a global market—be that a luxury goods conglomerate, a credit card company or a Hollywood star—calls in a stylist.

Magazine pages, however, still remain the launchpad of forward-thinking ideas. In magazines, great stylists are still allowed freedom to steer fashion in new directions. Authoritative players who also work as freelancers are now key team members at fashion shows, and their sphere of influence reaches far beyond backstage organization. In many cases, stylists are now designers' most trusted sounding boards. As consultants, creative directors, and design collaborators, they can shape the look of the clothes before they ever reach the runway, and then follow through by styling the advertising campaign.

Stylists who have risen to prominence at this rarefied level come, for the most part, from a fashion editing background, a tradition that stretches back to the dawn of photography in women's magazines (the term "stylist" first appeared in magazines in the 1930s). Though perhaps less significant in the smaller fashion industry of fifty years ago, the fashion editor's job of choosing clothes for readers to buy—and enjoy looking at—was always multifaceted. What set the great editor apart from the mundane one—then, as now—was not just a matter of a penetrating eye and the intelligence to "say" something in a set of pictures, but also the ability to form personal relationships with photographers, models, designers, and fashion houses. Those relationships of trust and like-mindedness always put the most important editors close to the creative center of the action in the inner sanctums of couture houses and the showrooms of Seventh Avenue as well as on the sets of the great fashion photographers. Today, stylists are more closely enmeshed with the rest of the fashion world than ever before.

But how did they arrive? Different stories emerge from each successive wave of talent, but, with few exceptions, they rose through the ranks, assisting senior stylists, or working for free on independent magazines or on the periphery of the music industry amongst close-knit friendship groups of young photographers and hair and makeup artists. The range of disciplines required to get anywhere doesn't vary, though. It arcs from the mundane skills of ironing, crease-free packing, and coffee-fetching right through to the advanced psychological skills of decision-making, persuasion, team-motivation, cheerleading, and—above all—the stubborn, motivating determination to realize a vision in pictures. At one end lies service journalism—styling fashion clearly and excitingly for readers to buy—and at the other, the grand, multipage style essay, a flight of imagination using fashion as an expressionistic tool. It may be romantic. It may be dark. It may be cinematic, literary, historical, satirical, or political—or, perhaps, soaringly happy. The distinguishing mark of a great stylist's work is the imagination that makes it something that could only come from one person's mind. Artistically respected, commercially effective, and intimately involved in the way the fashion world runs, their work is seen collected together within these pages for the first time.

SARAH MOWER

STYLIST

THE INTERPRETERS OF FASHION

POLLY MELLEN

Among the astonishing collection of landmark photographs in Polly Mellen's portfolio, one small snapshot sheds a rare sidelight on the taut intensity of the collaboration between a great fashion stylist and a great photographer. The photo catches Mellen in the studio with Richard Avedon sometime in the seventies. As Avedon lies half-prone on the floor, Mellen is tensed into an athletic crouch behind him, eyes locked in parallel with his, concentrating on critiquing, encouraging, and willing the image into being. "If you look at that photo," she says, "you see something of what it takes. It shows on my face; I'm rapt. Completely wrapped up in the experience."

Mellen was the fashion force on set when Avedon, Helmut Newton, and a roll call of other luminaries in photography produced some of their best work—images that belong to the exceptional class of fashion documentation that reaches the quality of psycho-sexual-sociopolitical commentary. Working for *Vogue*, Mellen conspired with Avedon to tune in with the mod youthquake and space-age futurism of the sixties. In the seventies she pushed the frontiers of sexual liberation alongside Newton. They are firsts: pictures that deploy chic, shock, and sex in such pared-down form that they still radiate a radical charge. As the retired Mellen observes today from her home in Connecticut, "I like to take things further. Too often stylists do things to please, because they are going to be accepted. You lose the magic that way. You can't give something special to your readers unless you dare. I was a stronger woman behind the camera than I was in real life. I dared."

With her signature white bob, tireless verve, and fearless capacity for modernity, Mellen occupies a unique position of renown in the fashion pantheon; however, for reasons of historical convention, even her most ardent admirers may not realize the full scope of the amazing work in which she was the invisible hand. When Mellen began her half-century-long career in 1950 as a well-turned-out Connecticut girl, she had arrived during the era in which the fashion editor—however vital her contribution to the picture—never saw her name attached to her work, and whose introduction to editing was a long haul through the accessory showrooms of Seventh Avenue. The young Mellen had spirit, though, and, after a stint as hat editor at *Mademoiselle*, she was propelled by family friend Sally Kirkland to an audience with Diana Vreeland, then the fashion editor at *Harper's Bazaar*. "I was totally smitten. Mrs. Vreeland was extraordinarily warm and wonderful. She'd tell me, 'The woman in Kansas can't afford couture, but the woman in Kansas can buy a paper pattern and work her way around it.' She believed in giving the reader escape and fantasy."

After putting in lowly groundwork as foundations editor, Mellen left *Harper's* to marry and to raise two young children. She returned to work with Vreeland at *Harper's Bazaar* as a fashion and sittings editor, and eventually moved on to *Vogue*, following Vreeland, who had become *Vogue*'s editor in chief. Mellen was right on time to throw her energy into the stylistic postwar clean sweep of the early sixties. With the young Avedon, she photographed one of Vreeland's biggest discoveries, the sixteen-year-old Penelope Tree. "She was the daughter of an ambassador to the UN, who had been brought up in a very progressive way. She was doing her makeup in this very intense way, with lots of eyeliner and mascara all around the eyes and with the rest of her face bare; she was all eyes and legs and still having growing pains. There was a childlike weirdness and honesty about her. I said 'Dick, you have to see her—she looks like she comes from outer space!'" They shot Tree shoeless in a Paraphernalia pantsuit ("I wanted it to look like a Beatle suit," Mellen recalls), and then, mesmerically, with feathered eyelashes in an Ungaro couture dress with a graphically curvilinear metal neckpiece. It is arguably one of the greatest fashion images of all time, freeze-framing all the shivery scientific hopes and fears of the unknown and the newly possible that ran through that American moment. "Dick was a total joy," Mellen says fondly. "He gave me such a growth of vision, imagination, and intellect. With him, it was always a conversation that involved you, a collaboration—and always fun."

The most incendiary of the many shoots that Mellen worked on was Helmut Newton's notorious "Story of Ohhh . . ."; it was one of the first depictions of proto-feminist sexuality from a woman's point of view to breach American mainstream media. Mellen's favorite shot is of Lisa Taylor, sitting with legs akimbo in a Calvin Klein dress and meeting the eye of a half-naked man; her expression is one of frank desire. "Helmut and I talked a lot on this shoot," she recalls. "The story for me was sex, heat, tease. The one where Lisa is sitting in the pool house—I got the position from seeing how women in Antigua would sit like that, with their legs apart. To make it work, the dress had to have simplicity. I put those ordinary raffia pool-slides on her feet. The little things made it less blatant, more interesting. People asked, 'Well . . . is it before or after?' For me," she laughs, "it's before, on the way to the action."

For Mellen, the buzz comes from pinpointing, at some level, a truth about the changing times and the vitality, sensuality, and complexity of the young women living them. For all the glamour and grandeur of the fashion shows, parties, and hoopla that her job involved—she was treated like royalty, leaving her final post as creative director of *Allure* and freelance styling, before retiring—Mellen's true gratification always came from that tense split second on set when the shutter would click and something amazing had been witnessed. "Oh, there were so many moments when I would just find tears running down my face," she says, and describes the day she and Avedon recorded Nastassja Kinski's naked encounter with a snake. "She laid down. The python started at her ankle, slowly moved up her body and then—*flick*!—kissed her ear. I mean, where else could you ever see something like that happen in front of you?"

Opposite:	Overleaf, left:	Overleaf, right:
Helmut Newton	Richard Avedon	Richard Avedon
Vogue	*Vogue*	*Vogue*
1975	1968	1967

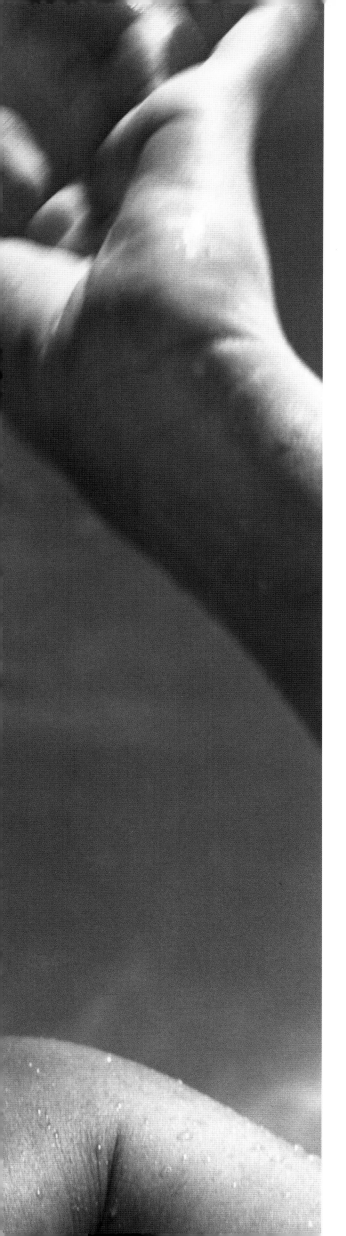

Opposite:
Richard Avedon
Vogue
1966

Overleaf:
Richard Avedon
Vogue
1981

This page and
opposite:
Behind-the-scenes
snapshots of Polly
Mellen on set in
Japan, and
collaborating with
Richard Avedon.

This page:
Helmut Newton
Vogue
1974

Opposite:
Helmut Newton
Vogue
1979

Overleaf:
Deborah Turbeville
Vogue
1975

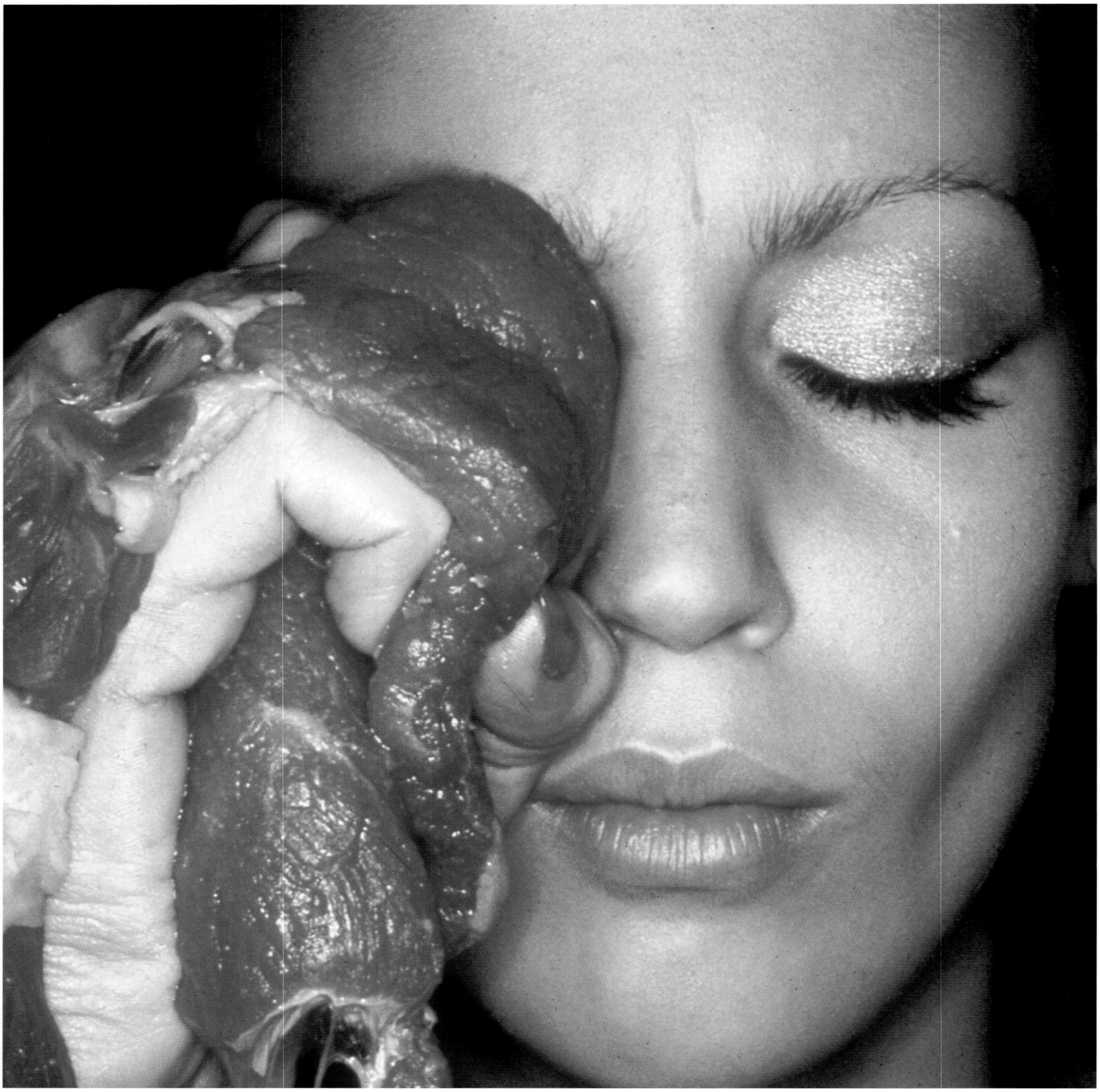

POLLY MELLEN

BORN
United States

LIVES IN
Connecticut

PHOTOGRAPHERS
Arthur Elgort, Helmut Newton, Irving Penn,
Richard Avedon, Steven Klein, Steven Meisel

PUBLICATIONS
Allure, Harper's Bazaar, Vogue

Opposite: Polly Mellen
photographed by
Steven Klein, 1997.
This page, clockwise
from top left: Polly as
a child; Polly as a
young girl with her
three siblings; an
Arthur Elgort snapshot
of Polly with three
models of the moment;
three impromptu
shots of Polly and
Richard Avedon.

CAMILLA NICKERSON

The first sight of a Camilla Nickerson story is always a jolt. Whatever clothes appear, the subtext is clearly operating beyond the normal conventions. "I try to show something new; the next thought," says this senior contributing fashion editor to *W* magazine. "The mantra here is 'If you've seen it before, don't do it.'" Nickerson's arresting work is the sort of allusive, content-laden material that ends up on designers' tackboards to be pored over as inspiration for the coming season. "I wouldn't like to think that I'm selling clothes." Rather than using the season's collections as a template for structuring her stories, Nickerson approaches her job from the other direction: "I try to bring in something from worlds that are outside fashion," she says, "and then try to relate fashion to it. I'm trying to think about the world today."

As a precocious seventeen-year-old Nickerson started working as a contributor to London style magazines. She has contributed to the British, Italian, and American editions of *Vogue*, becoming one of the many English fashion editors who migrated to New York in the nineties. Nickerson's distinctively intellectual approach frequently sparks connections with disturbing aspects of twenty-first-century consciousness. However fantastical or hallucinatory Nickerson's pictures seem at first glance, there's usually some sharp and timely political observation going on, as in the crazed, stylized depictions of implied violence and futuristic tension that she cooked up with Steven Meisel for Italian *Vogue*. Even an apparently simple Mario Sorrenti shoot depicting beautifully elegant fifties-influenced couture gowns is rendered tellingly melancholy (for there is no escape from the now) by the expression on Kate Moss's face. A religious reference—like the poetically disconcerting essay from 2004, showing an ethereal figure of the Virgin Mary—connects spirituality and morality to the plight of refugees, while also accurately predicting the shift from vulgar body exposure to modesty that was about to dominate fashion.

"You don't just turn up with the clothes," says Nickerson. "I don't know what other stylists do, but I bring boxes of images I've researched, so that everyone knows what I'm talking about." Her preparation can take weeks. She cites the example of the research that went into her Meisel story involving graffiti-scrawled, paint-daubed models. After discussing the idea with the photographer, she compiled tear sheets of Stephen Sprouse's splashy eighties freehand typography; pictures from a recent exhibition of street art she'd seen at Deitch Projects; punk reportage; surrealist and futurist art; and the society portraits of Nancy Cunard, Paula Gellibrand, and others. Then she talked it all over with the set designer, models, hairdresser, and makeup artist. Immersion in the multidimensional pile of references inspired everything from gestures to makeup and the plastic-wrap headpieces. As she puts it, "I make connections."

Nickerson's absorption in contemporary art and cinema runs parallel to her interest in aiding and abetting experiments with new digital photography technologies. An epic, noirish sci-fi story with Meisel was set in motion by Frank Miller's and Robert Rodriguez's 2005 film, *Sin City*, which pioneered a new animation technique. "I was just blown away by it. It had camera angles that were impossible; there was a hard futurism to it." The aim, though, is never to mimic sources literally. "What you're always waiting for," she says, "is that lovely moment when something you could never imagine happens on the set."

If Nickerson's unorthodox approach seems at a sharp tangent to the work of designers, her respect for what they do is profound. "They are masters—extraordinary animals," she believes. "I am floored by the ability to be so in line with your craft and then to make an idea so fluent on a runway."

Behind the scenes, her razor-sharp eye for modernity won her a consultancy with Narciso Rodriguez in New York, and, more recently, with Stefano Pilati at Yves Saint Laurent in 2004. Whether she's working with designers or photographers, however, it's Nickerson's humility about the relative value of her creative contribution that is striking. "I don't think we, as stylists, have a patch on them. You're the shopper, not the chef. I have the great luck to work with masters. I always feel I'm learning. After all these years, I often feel I'm just there as a pupil."

Opposite:
Mario Sorrenti
W
2005

Overleaf:
Steven Meisel
Italian *Vogue*
2005

INSPIRATION

In Nickerson's shoot for Italian *Vogue*, photographed by Steven Meisel in 2005 (previous and opposite pages), she incorporated bold text, influenced by Christopher Wool's word paintings (an example from 1991, above left). The cellophane used in Cecil Beaton's photograph for *Vogue*, above right, was reinvented by Nickerson as a dynamic, moving element in the same story; and the visually confrontational tone of Richard Pandiscio's image of Stephen Sprouse, left, photographed for *Paper* magazine in 1987, defined the mood for the shoot.

INSPIRATION

Sin City, the 2005 film based on Frank Miller's comic book series, was the jumping-off point for Nickerson's foray into highly technological fashion photography. Above and at right are two film stills from the movie that influenced Nickerson's collaboration with Steven Meisel for a 2005 Italian *Vogue* shoot, opposite.

Pages 30–31:
Juergen Teller
W
2007

Opposite:
Juergen Teller
YSL
advertising campaign
2005

This page:
Yves Saint Laurent
Rive Gauche by
Stefano Pilati, spring
2005 ready-to-wear.
Photography by
Marcio Madeira/
Style.com

INSPIRATION

Cecil Beaton's 1927 photograph of his sister, Baba, left, for *Vogue*, turns subject matter, clothing, and setting into a nearly seamless whole, just as Nickerson's collaboration with photographer Nick Knight in the 2005 *W* story "Altered States," opposite, transforms dress and wearer into one.

German surrealist Max Ernst's *Anatomy of the Bride*, 1921, bottom right, pushed Nickerson to look at the human form as a mutable entity.

This decidedly unfashionable plastic mummy, bottom left, also shaped Nickerson's mindset for "Altered States." Tension and ambiguity are central to both works.

CAMILLA NICKERSON

BORN
England

LIVES IN
New York

PHOTOGRAPHERS
David Sims, Helmut Newton, Inez van Lamsweerde
and Vinoodh Matadin, Juergen Teller, Mario Sorrenti,
Mario Testino, Steven Klein, Steven Meisel

PUBLICATIONS
Vogue, W

Opposite: Camilla
Nickerson photographed
by Inez van Lamsweerde
and Vinoodh Matadin
for *W*. This page:
Nickerson's home and
the stylist with her son,
all photographed by
Todd Eberle for *Vogue*
in 1999.

CARINE ROITFELD

Carine Roitfeld, editor in chief of French *Vogue*, arguably the most fiercely chic woman in European fashion, declares, "I am not a good professional of fashion. I am not an expert about how clothes are constructed or the history of fashion. I never start with fashion. I always think of the girl and her personality—because all that matters to me when you look at a page is, 'Do you want to be that girl?'"

Roitfeld's unwavering adherence to tight, knee-length skirts, high heels, rod-straight hair with bangs in her eyes created a look—part raw rock chick, part slick Parisienne—that, through her work as a stylist for Tom Ford at Gucci, became iconic. It was Roitfeld who, working in a closely knit team with Ford and photographer Mario Testino, helped usher in the sex-and-glamour advertising imagery that took Gucci from bankruptcy to boom in the nineties. Sometimes Roitfeld's own clothes would be duplicated in Ford's collection. (One hot day she went to a shoot in stiletto slingbacks with the straps hanging over the back of the heel; later this look was transformed into a Gucci shoe designed to be worn that way.) In 2005, the Carine Roitfeld style crossed over still further when Kalman Ruttenstein, late fashion director at Bloomingdale's, commissioned advertisements featuring models styled to look like her.

In many ways, Roitfeld personifies a mystery many women can never work out: the fact that, although Paris is the capital of international fashion, the place where the most extravagant fantasias and avant-garde breakthroughs are created and made—and available—the Frenchwoman never swallows it whole. "I love to surprise in a picture," Roitfeld says, "but in a simple way. It's about how you push up your sleeve, or knowing the right moment to wear a Chanel bag." In the Parisian order of things, what matters far more than mere transient fashion is a woman's own instinctual style. "For me, when I'm looking at a show, I ask, 'Do I like it or not?'," says Roitfeld, meaning that her eye never hovers objectively over a collection with intellectual intent. "When I have an idea it's always spontaneous—that I have to add white shoes or open a button. It's a feeling."

The twist is that Roitfeld is only half French. Her father, Jacques Roitfeld, was Russian, a movie producer whose distinctly glamorous influence shaped her life. "He was very chic: it's an attitude. This is a gift. You can learn not to make mistakes, but you cannot learn to be chic." Her mother brought *Elle* home and Carine would scan every story weekly. "But fashion was not for teenagers in Paris in the sixties and seventies," she remembers. "We went to Clignancourt Flea Market, where I found army surplus clothes and my first bell-bottoms—which had fringes below the knee! And when I went to London I came back with velvet trousers and T-shirts."

After a fleeting stint as a junior model, Roitfeld worked as a writer on the "Idées-Elle" news pages at the back of the weekly magazine, contributing pieces on how to be a model, or how to get a tattoo, which no one did in those days. Perhaps the Russian side of her character provided the daring to see things differently than a girl from a straightforward bon chic, bon genre background. "I think I am more open-minded. In France they don't take risks." Roitfeld went from styling beauty pictures to working with Jean-Baptiste Mondino on some of his strong, androgynous early-eighties images, often pushing shoots to the point even of being fired. "Once we did a story with a model whose hair was clipped like a man's, wearing Doc Martens, sitting in the street. It looks normal now, but the client did not like that."

Though it is unusual for a *Vogue* editor in chief, Roitfeld has kept shooting since her appointment in 2001, but, she says, the impulse toward a new gesture or detail seldom comes from the runway. "Seeing beautifully dressed women wearing the season's latest clothes never inspires me. What can I learn from them? Sometimes I'm more inspired sitting in an airport lounge. I like to look at people. I like errors. I love high heels with jogging pants; black lingerie under white T-shirts. The mistakes."

After meeting and moving in with Christian Restoin, a successful shirt manufacturer and retailer, and having two children, Julie and Vladimir, Roitfeld freelanced for European editions of Condé Nast magazines. French *Glamour*, aimed at young fashion fanatics, was an outlet for some of her more prescient ideas. She recalls *Glamour* as being a great laboratory for fashion where everything was possible. For one story, she prefigured the shrunken T-shirt trend of the early nineties by putting children's Lacoste polo shirts and XX-small soccer shirts on grown models. In another, she took Helena Christensen to Peru, mixing high fashion with her father's Peruvian sweaters and cheap jelly shoes. A third shoot, she relates, was a turning point in her career. "Mario and I photographed Nadja Auermann in my apartment as a very blonde, very sexy bourgeoisie—a new idea of sexy. There was one shot where she was pulling her T-shirt under her miniskirt. And we had Gucci loafers in the story." Tom Ford saw it, called Roitfeld and Testino and, by force of charm (because they didn't know who he was) persuaded them to shoot his first advertising campaign in 1995. "That," she says, "is what gave us Gucci."

Ford, Testino, and Roitfeld saw eye to eye. "All the Gucci campaigns were about sensuality," she says. "It was the beginning of porno-chic." As it escalated, some of the steamiest shoots involved couples, apparent orgies, shoes with bondage straps, snakes. Roitfeld laughs that there should be no misunderstandings. "It's just my imagination that goes into my pictures. I was never a punk. Never dyed my hair blue. Never a nymphomaniac. I'm a married woman with children," she insists. "But I don't like the girl next door."

Opposite and overleaf:
Mario Testino
The Face
1998

This page and
opposite:
Mario Testino
French *Glamour*
1993

This page and
opposite:
Mario Testino
French *Glamour*
1994

This page:
Gucci by Tom Ford,
fall 1995 ready-to-
wear. Photography by
Dan Lecca

Opposite:
Mario Testino
Gucci
advertising campaign
1995

Overleaf:
Mario Testino
French *Vogue*
2005

CARINE ROITFELD

BORN
France

LIVES IN
Paris

PHOTOGRAPHERS
Jean-Baptiste Mondino, Mario Testino

PUBLICATIONS
French Glamour, French Vogue

CAMPAIGNS
Gucci

Opposite: Carine
Roitfeld photographed
by Inez van Lamsweerde
and Vinoodh Matadin
for *V*, March 2003. This
page, clockwise from
top left: Roitfeld and
her staff; Roitfeld as a
young girl; Roitfeld with
Christian Restoin and
their children, Julia
and Vladimir; Roitfeld's
inspiration board;
an interior shot of
Roitfeld's home.

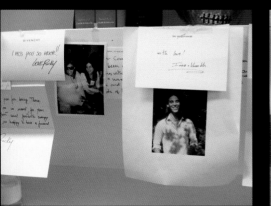

GRACE CODDINGTON

To see Grace Coddington at a show is to watch one of fashion's great poker players in session. There she is in the front row: blazing hair, dark coat, white shirt, narrow pants and sandals, eyes barely leaving the runway as her hand moves relentlessly across the pages of her leather-bound sketchbook. By the end, every single look is noted in outline, but not a single reaction will have registered on her face. Was that collection good? Mediocre? Irredeemable? To the disappointment of those who seek a lead (and designers' minions watching from the wings) there is never the slightest clue as to what the creative director of American *Vogue* is thinking, or exactly which pieces her assistant may be calling in as she leaves the building.

Coddington is the personification of old-school British reticence, but maintaining an aloof demeanor has little to do with her concerns at a show: simply, her mind's eye is probably not on what other people are seeing. "At shows, I do find 'trends' very dull. Spots and stripes? Parkas? Urban sport? That bores me," she shrugs. Where others might be looking for "sixties space-age," Coddington will be on the lookout for Marie Antoinette gowns to shoot at Versailles, or tracking blue when everyone else is talking up beige. One season, it was a specific Alice-in-Wonderland blue, as illustrated by John Tenniel, for a spectacular December 2005 fantasia involving the baby-faced Russian model Natalia Vodianova, major designers as extras, and a crew large enough for a small movie. She selects this as one of her all-time favorite sittings (which, in an editing career that began in 1968, is saying a great deal). "I'm a narrative editor," she declares. "That's not all I do—I love very clear, totally defined fashion pictures, as well. I like flicking between the two. But either way," she remarks, typically sticklerish, "I think it's a sin if you can't see the clothes."

Looking through Coddington's favorite work (her tome, *Grace: Thirty Years of Fashion at Vogue*, is a good place to start) reveals a peerless record of every significant nuance of design, from Yves Saint Laurent chubbies in the seventies to Calvin Klein's streamlined eighties; Marc Jacobs's grunge in the nineties to millennial bling and beyond. Still, what's striking, through the 180-degree swings in fashion and the vastly different stylistic imprints of photographers, is the witty, playful, whimsical Coddington Girl at the heart of every picture. In her serial adventures (sometimes alone, often in pairs, bevies and gangs, and frequently frolicking with the handsomest guys) she is identifiable throughout. Her presence is testament to Coddington's strength of personality—a talent that goes far deeper into the picture than the mere selection of lovely clothes. Coddington has virtually produced a genre of her own: fashion documentary with a skittish humanity that sparkles decades after the dress has faded into history.

Asked to define how she does that, Coddington will only say what motivates her is "feeling the girl" in a picture, and "how one wishes people would look in their going-along lives." Inspiration can come from all directions— not necessarily clothes but life, close to home. She took Steven Klein to shoot a surreal story in the New York apartment Vodianova shares with her husband, Justin Portman, and their baby son, in which mom is painted silver because she is running out to a Halloween party. For a shoot with Daria Werbowy, Coddington was happy to build "boring but wearable" clothes into a story about boxing that referenced the sixties; it evolved from thinking about a Gary Winogrand photograph of a boxer in Central Park, Hilary Swank in *Million Dollar Baby*, and the fact that Coddington's partner, Didier Malige, watches boxing on television at home. Another story, which opened with Amber Valletta sitting on a plastic-covered sofa, was triggered by Coddington's annoyance at the encroachments of the communication age. "People don't ever speak to each other anymore," she objects, "only by computer, phone, BlackBerry. It was really getting to me. In restaurants you see lovers sitting with their BlackBerrys—each talking to someone else on the phone. I also thought about that movie *Safe*, in which Julianne Moore is allergic to everything. I took it a stage further and it became an anti-germ thing, about isolation."

She has never much considered where she got her vividly visual storytelling imagination. At home in Anglesey (an island off northern Wales), where Coddington was born to hoteliers in 1941, she doesn't remember reading stories, and was never read to. So who is that fashion-loving fun-life girl who runs serially through all of her pictures? Surely it's Grace herself, who escaped dour Wales to win a *Vogue* modeling competition in soon-to-be Swinging London in 1959. From time to time, a red-headed Gracelet turns up in her pictures, most notably in the form of Karen Elson and Maggie Rizer in the nineties, and lately as the doll-faced ginger-haired English model Lily Cole, who is an uncannily exact double of Coddington in her early-seventies glam-rock mode. "Yes, I see myself in Lily," she laughs, "though she's far prettier than I was. I like pale skin. I don't like pretty-pretty classic beauty. I don't really like sexy either."

For anyone who knows the history of fashion, the nimbus of hair, white skin, and giant eyes harks directly back to photographs of Coddington herself in the sixties and seventies as a model in British *Vogue*. It was there that she made the transition to fashion editor in 1968, leaping the Atlantic twenty years later to become creative director at American *Vogue* in 1988. There was a short interlude in between, when she served as creative director at Calvin Klein but, as much as she loved the designer, it didn't work. As she puts it, "I just couldn't keep away from the pages," she says, "and here I am: still hoping to do the perfect picture, and never satisfied."

Opposite:
Arthur Elgort
Vogue
2003

Pages 54–57:
Annie Leibovitz
Vogue
2003

This page and
opposite:
Craig McDean
Vogue
2002

Overleaf:
Steven Meisel
Vogue
2006

Pages 62–65:
Steven Klein
Vogue
2003

GRACE CODDINGTON

BORN
Wales

LIVES IN
New York

PHOTOGRAPHERS
Annie Leibovitz, Arthur Elgort, Bruce Weber, Craig McDean, David Sims, Ellen von Unwerth, Helmut Newton, Steven Klein, Steven Meisel, Tim Walker

PUBLICATIONS
British Vogue, Vogue

CAMPAIGNS
Calvin Klein Eternity (as design director)

Opposite:
Grace Coddington photographed by Steven Meisel, 1992. This page: a collage of images from Grace's storied life among the fashion elite.

KARL TEMPLER

Whatever forces of physicality and hipness whip out of a Karl Templer layout, it's rarely the fashion that hits first. That may sound like an odd contradiction in the work of a sought-after fashion stylist, but it's central to the calculated, masculine viewpoint of Templer's work. "I'm interested in the schematics of every detail in an image," he explains, "and what they allow you to read into the character." Those characters are often half-naked players in off-limits dramas that spill across the pages of Italian *Vogue*, French *Vogue*, *L'Uomo Vogue*, *W*, or *Arena Homme Plus*.

In a Templer shoot, "reality" will come first, fashion second: minute bikini bottoms or sea-soaked jeans stick to oil-slicked bodies; shirts and shorts are thrown together by gangs of teen renegades; women get slammed on car windshields by security-crazed cops.

This apparently low-intervention method is, of course, just the opposite, since Templer's casualness is executed with fanatical perfectionism—a characteristic he traces to his beginnings as a freelance menswear editor in Britain. "Girls have so much to choose from in fashion, and it's different every season," he observes, "but for men, fashion is always about the importance of much smaller changes: whether a jacket has one button or two; if there's one vent, two, or none. I was always more interested in the authenticity of an item, in underground cool, and what a piece of clothing would mean to your peer group. I think I know about popular culture and the visual history of things—what each item signifies from the details. And maybe I see the bigger picture."

The ability to mix clothes unobtrusively into a wider context has brought Templer significant advertising commissions from Calvin Klein, Hugo Boss, and Benetton, all brands requiring global images that resonate beyond passing seasonal trends. Like other stylists working at this level, Templer's behind-the-scenes role often involves consultations on design. "What I am is a professional second opinion," he says. "If you do an advertising shoot in America, there will be a tailor on set so you can tweak the clothes, refine things, make them better-looking. What I've learned is restraint, control, subtlety. And to concentrate on what the client needs."

Templer moved to New York in 1998, a decade after styling his first small stories in London for *The Face*, the original eighties style bible that merged street fashion with international designer clothes, bringing slick, groundbreaking photography to a youth audience. Templer was at school with the children of Nick Logan, the magazine's founder. "Reading *The Face* at the age of twelve or thirteen was my first introduction to fashion," he recalls. "I was always asking the Logans, 'How do you do it?'"

In 1985 Templer got a job as a shop assistant at Woodhouse, a store in London's Covent Garden that, at the time, was setting the pace in men's designer fashion. "I started to see a bit of how the industry operated there, because stylists for print advertising and commercials would come in and borrow clothes. There was an explosion of menswear—Jean Paul Gaultier was big; Comme des Garçons was beginning; clubs like Taboo, where Leigh Bowery would dress up, were going on," he remembers. "But I wasn't part of that major fashion thing. I came from the suburbs; I wanted to stand out without standing out, so I was interested in the iconic value of things that already existed. Most of the things that are cool now—loafers, biker jackets, Levi's, Converse—have always been cool; they had value before they were touched by designers. They were already 'right.'"

While he was acquiring an encyclopedic knowledge of authentic brands, Templer found himself mesmerized by the naturalistic, narrative, American fashion imagery of Bruce Weber, which was appearing in *The Face* and Italian and British editions of *Vogue*. "I was quite aware of wanting to live that dream. And very conscious of the American way—Calvin Klein's and Ralph Lauren's way—of selling you a vision. It was iconic, about branding. It was so visual, very different from the European way. I was such a visual person, getting off on the image."

Templer moved steadily into major editorial commissions, as well as long stints as a freelance editor at *L'Uomo Vogue* and *Arena Homme Plus*. By the time he arrived in the States, it was almost a spiritual homecoming. "In America it was a very different thing. You get paid! You realize it's not about talking to fifteen people you know in East London—it's about communicating to a much bigger audience." In 1997 he graduated to doing women's shoots, clicking into what he sees as fashion's "gradual shift to 'item culture'"—the increasing fixation on bags and other accessories that took off with the millennium. Templer also notes fashion's enduring fondness for historical references. "Designers are restyling the past, and stylists are restyling images from the past," he says. "It's part of the vintage thing." That, of course, finds him on solid ground, in the heritage territory he's always known. Even so, he still prefers to work in semi-obscurity. "I've always thought it should be about the work, not about me. I don't have a set role or type of story that I do. Everything's a compromise," he muses. "I'll be presented with a set of variables—clothes that have to be shot for different reasons, and my way of looking at it is, 'Can I fulfill all the criteria and still have something to say?' That's when I feel an idea's really well done."

Opposite:
Steven Klein
Arena Homme Plus
2001

This page and
opposite:
Fabien Baron
W
2000

Overleaf:
Mikael Jansson
Arena Homme Plus
2000

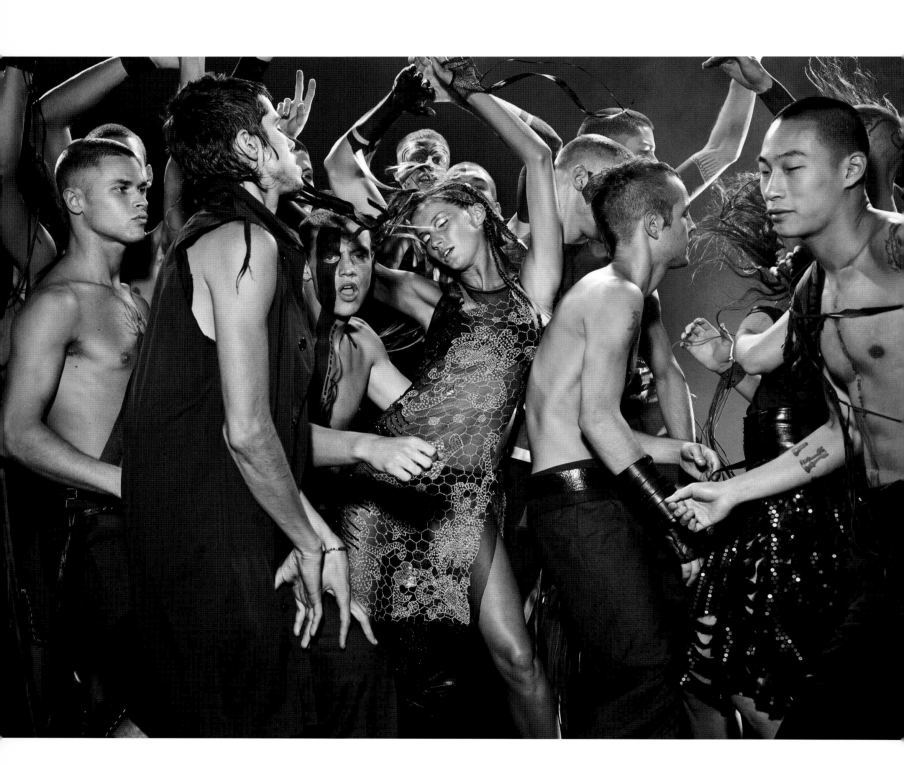

This page and
opposite:
David Sims
W
2004

This page:
David Sims
French *Vogue*
2007

Opposite:
David Sims
French *Vogue*
2005

This page and
opposite:
Mikael Jansson
Pop
2005

Overleaf:
Mikael Jansson
Arena Homme Plus
2001

KARL TEMPLER

BORN
England

LIVES IN
New York

PHOTOGRAPHERS
Craig McDean, David Sims, Fabien Baron, Mario Sorrenti,
Mikael Jansson, Peter Lindbergh, Steven Klein,
Steven Meisel

PUBLICATIONS
French Vogue, Italian Vogue, L'Uomo Vogue, Japanese Vogue,
V, W

CAMPAIGNS
Asprey, Benetton, Burberry, Calvin Klein, Gap, Gucci,
Hugo Boss, Nicole Farhi, Tod's

Opposite: Karl Templer
photographed by
Mikael Jansson for *W*.
This page, top: Templer
on set, photographed
by Peter Lindbergh;
middle: Christina Kruse
with her and Templer's
son, August; bottom:
Templer's living room.

ALEX WHITE

Even in a room full of other work, an Alex White shoot would stand out for its tight, graphic composition, high points of saturated color, and the uncompromisingly sensual fantasy girl in the frame. "I like to present women in a very strong, sexual way," says White. "I'm a big fan of tutus, ballet tights, and great shoes. And I really love color. I suppose my thing is always slightly about dressing like a little girl—but with breasts. I never think the girl looks submissive."

Another giveaway would be the scale of the tear sheets in White's portfolio. The ten-by-thirteen-inch format—larger than mainstream magazines—belongs to *W*, the insider fashion/beauty/lifestyle/society monthly that has carved a unique niche as a luxury image lab alongside its news-based parent publication, *Women's Wear Daily*. White was appointed fashion director in 2003, but she has been a contributing fashion editor since *W*'s chairman and editorial director, Patrick McCarthy, and its creative director, Dennis Freedman, transformed the magazine in 1993 by introducing the new glossy format, an editorial policy that set the magazine on course as a high-level fashion influencer.

White offers her "Polaroid books"—a collection of scrapbooks into which she has pasted preliminary shots over the years—as a more detailed explanation of her evolution as a stylist. Seen together, they form an incidental diary of the fashion of the times and, even more strongly, as a record of White's knack for magicking a seamlessly high-end image out of avant-garde clothes and a strange setting. "I used to love making these little books. I kept them because they made an ideal record of what we'd done, and because I always work on the layout with the photographer; we'd sit together and figure out the sequence, then I'd take it back to show the art director."

White's scrapbooks begin in the mid-nineties, when she'd recently moved to New York from London as a freelancer, contributing to *The Face*, Italian *Vogue*, and *W*. They show sequences of magazine shoots by Craig McDean, Mario Sorrenti, David Sims, Glen Luchford, Mert Alas and Marcus Piggott, Inez van Lamsweerde and Vinoodh Matadin, and Mario Testino alongside snapshots from the making of the definitive mid-decade global advertising campaigns for Prada (with Luchford) and Burberry (with Testino) that positioned those brands as rising powerhouses in the nineties.

A child of the eighties, whose first fashion memory is reading the pop magazine *FAB 208* after having her tonsils removed, White broke into styling through an internship at British *Elle*, and through booking models, photographers, and everything else while running Kim Knott's photography studio. She later graduated from booking models at *Harpers & Queen* to the magazine's fashion department. Come the early nineties, White joined the influx of young British stylists moving into the upper echelons of New York magazines. If that seems a long way from her origins as a Hertfordshire convent-school girl, it is—but it's not so very far that her roots don't show. "I was a ballet-mad girl with a bedroom plastered with magazine pages," she shrugs. "I suppose that says it all."

White's shoots are multi-sourced fantasias, often realized with the use of custom-made props and pieces of clothing. "Generally, I get a lot of inspiration from traveling and watching people, and now from my children. But I never know exactly how things are going to evolve on set," she says. She cites an Inez van Lamsweerde swimwear story that was pushed into the realm of glamorous sci-fi: "It was like *Barbarella*, Russ Meyer, Greek goddess, and *Power Rangers* rolled into one. I had shiny plastic headpieces made by Peter Phillips that reminded me of the pink Power Ranger." The potential for another typical collision of the playful and the erotic hit White when she took her children to a water park. "It was a childlike location. I had pink rubber inflatables made as props and latex leggings to match, and the skirts were short, with under-frills."

During the late nineties White's eye for childlike chic emerged, too, in her work behind the scenes at Prada and Burberry. "I was at Prada for two and a half years. I'll never forget my first show, when Kate Moss went out in a gray V-neck sweater and a pair of flannel pants, like a schoolgirl. But Miuccia had taken it to a luxury level I'd never seen before." For Burberry's advertising, White collaborated with Testino and art director Fabien Baron to create British "family" narratives at a time when the brand—and the fashionableness of its check—was in the initial stages of a major overhaul by the CEO, Rose Marie Bravo. "It was really exciting to make something new out of it; we had all sorts of clothes and accessories made for us, because at that time the collection didn't really exist," she recalls. During one of five seasons that she styled for Marc Jacobs at Louis Vuitton, White put her stamp on the introduction of the company's best-selling Takashi Murakami bags by suggesting they should be toted by girls wearing satin beauty-therapists' coats, cutely referencing the Parisian salon Carita, in the pastel colors of macaroons from the haute pâtisserie, Ladurée.

The creative license given by *W* allows White to showcase extreme fashion from young designers (like her compatriots Alexander McQueen, Giles Deacon, and Gareth Pugh), but always in the context of clothes, jewelry, and accessories from more established sources. That combination—and the deliberate, polished quality of the pages—has put *W*'s style in a category of its own. As rarefied as that look has become, White insists she only learned her skills by working out how to make dismal clothes look appetizing. "My first shoot as a junior fashion editor at *Harpers & Queen* was a special offer—German fashion, available to readers at a discount. I was glad; it prepares you."

Opposite:
Mert Alas and
Marcus Piggott
W
2005

Overleaf:
Inez van Lamsweerde
and Vinoodh Matadin
W
2006

INSPIRATION

Jean Harlow defined
Hollywood glamour in
her day. These iconic
1930s photographs of the
"Platinum Blonde," shot
by photographer George
Hurrell, led White to
create her own Harlow,
opposite, for a 2004
W magazine shoot
photographed by Mert
Alas and Marcus Piggott.

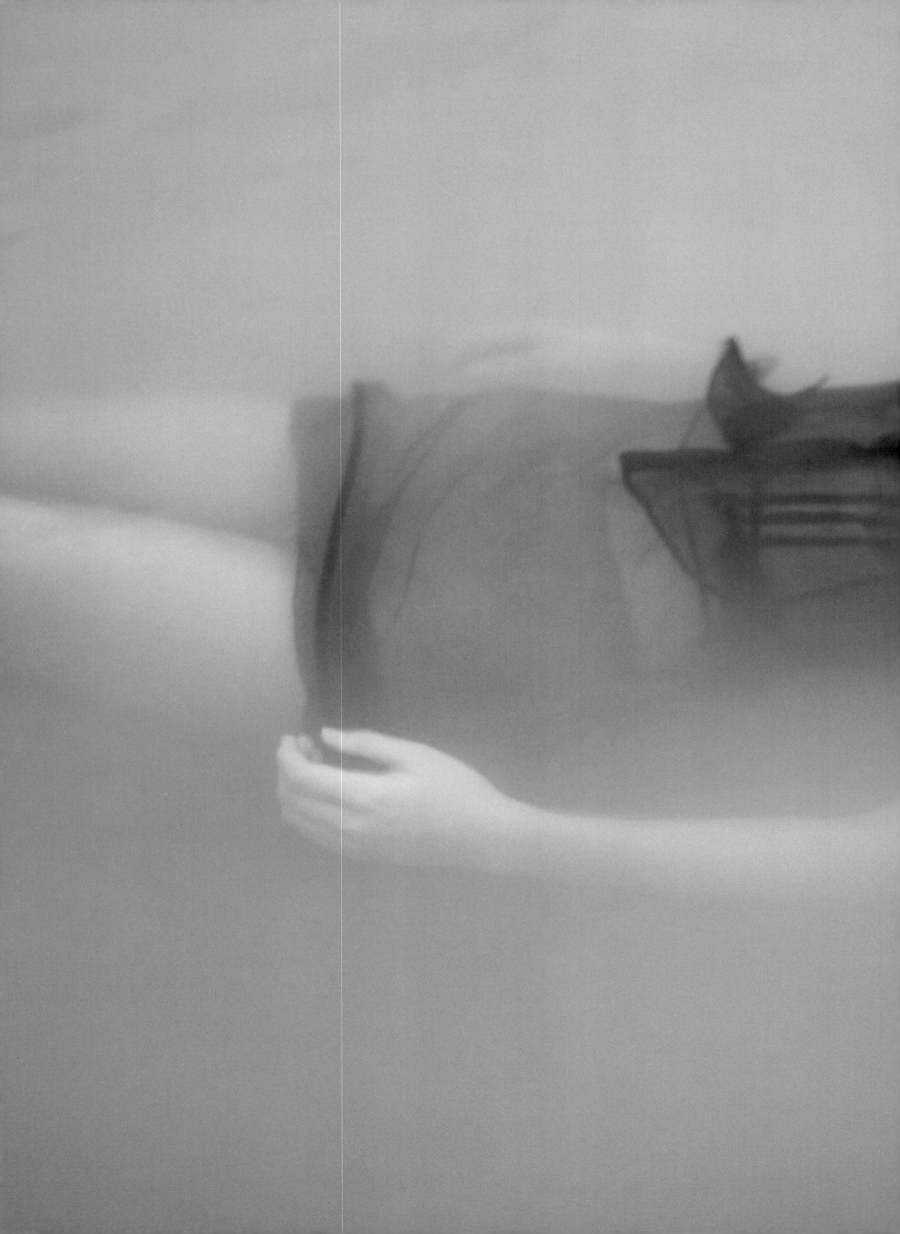

Pages 90–91:   This page: Opposite:
Glen Luchford   Inez van Lamsweerde   Craig McDean
Prada   and Vinoodh Matadin   W
advertising campaign W   2001
1997   2000

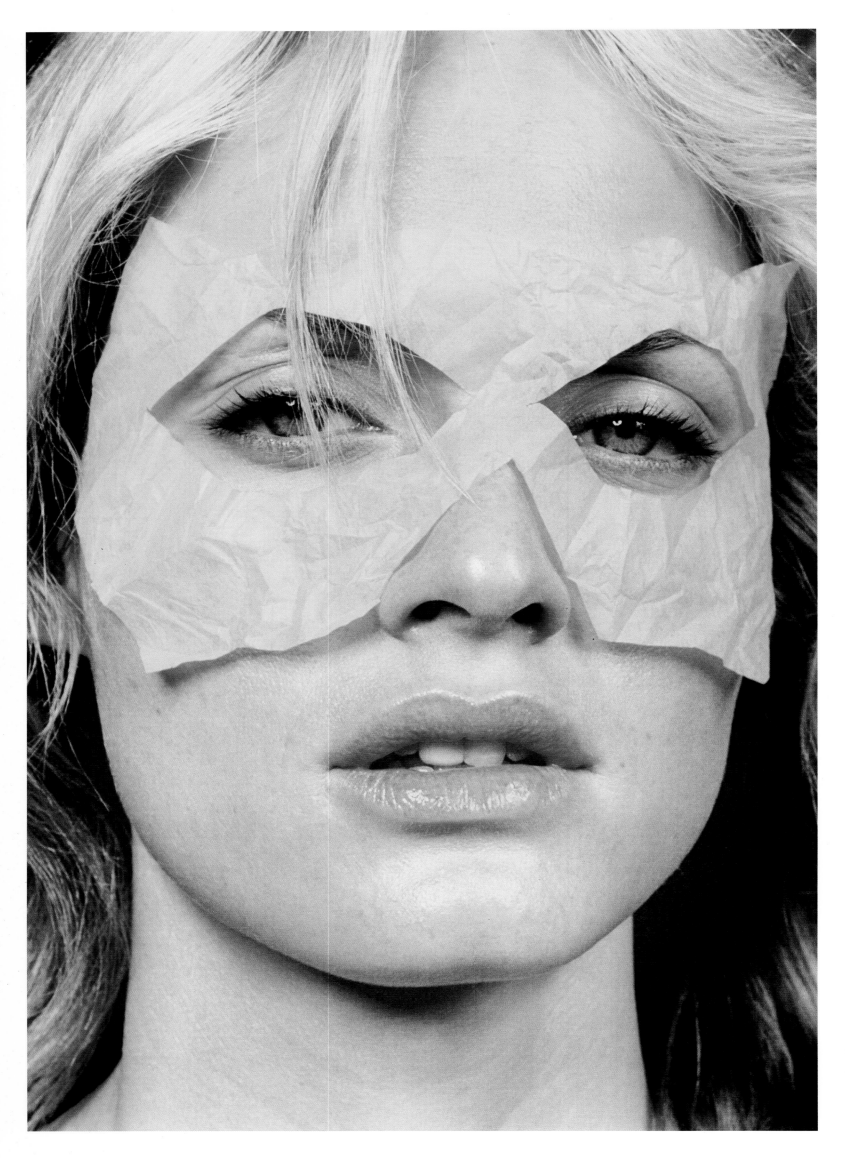

Opposite:
Craig McDean
Yohji Yamamoto
advertising campaign
2000/2001

This page:
Louis Vuitton by
Marc Jacobs, fall 2004
ready-to-wear.
Photography by
Marcio Madeira/
Style.com

ALEX WHITE

BORN
England

LIVES IN
New York

PHOTOGRAPHERS
Bruce Weber, Craig McDean, David Sims, Dusan Reljin, Inez van Lamsweerde and Vinoodh Matadin, Juergen Teller, Karl Lagerfeld, Mario Sorrenti, Mario Testino, Mert Alas and Marcus Piggott, Michael Thompson, Paolo Roversi, Tim Walker

PUBLICATIONS
Italian Vogue, W

CAMPAIGNS
Burberry, Calvin Klein, Chanel, David Yurman, Giorgio Armani, Louis Vuitton, Prada

Opposite: Alex White, portrait by Mert Alas and Marcus Piggott, 2007. This page, top: White (center, standing) on location in Niagra Falls with her fashion crew, including, from left to right, makeup artist Lucia Pieroni, hairstylist Eugene Souleiman; model Guinevere van Seenus, and photographer Craig McDean; middle: White with her husband, Shaheen Knox, shot on location in Goa, India; bottom: White celebrates her birthday with son, Harrison, and daughter, India.

MELANIE WARD

Melanie Ward is one of a cohort of soft-spoken subversives whose young, London-led realism provoked the sweeping overhaul of fashion in the 1990s. "In the early days, we were reacting against everything that was maximal and super-perfect," she says of the gang who cracked the glossy facade of establishment fashion, defined the term "edgy," and eventually found themselves placed high up in the New York fashion world as leaders of minimalism. It was to become the official style that dominated the decade.

It began in London among a loose coalition of friends linked by beginner photographers Corinne Day, Nigel Shafran, David Sims, and Craig McDean. "It was a time of recession," says Ward. "You made things up for yourself." High fashion, then dominated by supermodels, power shoulders, and big hair was, to Ward and her generation, an alien universe scarcely worth a derisory glance. Instead, they turned their cameras inward on their own world of penniless teen living, concocting pictures which surfaced, unpaid for, in British street-style magazines *The Face* and *i-D*.

In this freestyle, squat-and-bedsit culture, anyone with a sewing kit and an idea could help out with the clothes. Ward, who as a girl attended a school run by a convent and who had a politics and languages degree from London University, came qualified with a lifelong mania for fashion. "As a child, I was always customizing things, ruining my mother's saucepans by dyeing things black in them; taking over my aunt's sewing machine to change the clothes I'd bought at Oxfam and Portobello," she recalls. "I'd cut holes; twist sweaters into something else. I bought a man's jacket and wore it as a mini-dress to a club. For me, there were no rules, and that's still my belief."

One summer morning in 1989, Ward drove to the seaside with her photographer friend Corinne Day and a skinny fifteen-year-old named Kate Moss. This group of young female talent was to shake the fashion world. Ward made a daisy-chain necklace and put a five-dollar Native American feather headdress on Kate, who giggled into the sun, showing freckles and a snaggletooth. Day shot some rolls of black and white. "The pictures were raw; no makeup, in a hard light—gritty and un-retouched—with a model who didn't look like a model," Ward remembers. "I always wanted to make people look as if they were wearing their own clothes."

The most precious quality those spontaneous, carefree images of Moss possessed was authenticity. *The Face* used them for a moment-defining cover story announcing "The Second Summer of Love." Everyone under twenty-five in England recognized exactly what it meant. Illegal raves were taking place in fields all over the country, with Ecstasy-popping teenagers dancing all night in old jeans and T-shirts, long skirts, beat-up sneakers, flip-flops, and Birkenstocks. The unknown girl on the cover was clearly one of them; it was a generation rebelling and reveling in its unvarnished sense of freedom. Charged with a beautiful and shocking freshness, images like this hit high fashion with a force that made it look instantly old, fake, and outdated.

Ward's naturalistic shoots often subsumed fashion into social documentary, adding a sly, sometimes sexual subtext. "Nigel Shafran and I would photograph teenagers hanging around shopping precincts, or ask old ladies to dress up in Louis Vuitton," she recalls. Ward forged a bond with David Sims, the assistant to influential *i-D* photographer Nick Knight. "David and I both work with character and we're inspired by the imperfect," says Ward. "There was often a sense of pathos and irony in what we did. Some of it was a little voyeuristic, like watching kids play dress-up," she admits.

Two highly influential fashion figures were watching Melanie Ward's credits. One, Helmut Lang, a new Austrian designer who was beginning to show his collection in Paris, wrote her a fan letter requesting that she help style his show. The other was Calvin Klein. His creative director, Ronnie Cooke Newhouse, contacted Ward to work on the groundbreaking jeans campaign that would make Kate Moss a phenomenon in America. "Calvin was the first to pick up on us," says Ward. "He embraced new talent and trusted you without micromanaging."

The start of Ward's relationships with Lang and Klein is the point where her improvisational styling talents began to shape the design of clothes. In the mid-nineties, when she shot for Klein, there was no such thing as skinny hipster jeans. She took Calvin's men's jeans, cut out the waistband, and stapled them up the back like leggings. Then she would wet and grease them, and get an army of people to sandpaper them; inventing all the distressed-denim techniques that would soon become commonplace. Working alongside Lang, Ward plotted the evolution of the narrow, black, man-tailored pants that became his signature. They were based, Ward-style, on a piece of "found" British clothing: a pair of boy's trousers from the school uniform department of London store John Lewis.

In 1995 Ward moved to New York, hired by Liz Tilberis at *Harper's Bazaar*, a magazine that was showcasing a swathe of British photographers—David Sims and Craig McDean included—who were scrubbing off the London grime and turning the look into a stark, new, internationally intelligible definition of elegance. By now, London's anti-fashion gang were the grown-ups, creating the visual environment in which the minimalist clothes designed by Calvin Klein, Helmut Lang, Jil Sander, Prada, and Ann Demeulemeester looked right. Lang moved from Vienna to New York, where Ward collaborated with him until 2005; together they merged a cool, sophisticated, couture-informed sense of luxury into his urban street uniform.

Ward continues to live and work in New York as a senior fashion editor at *Harper's Bazaar*, regarding her work with an essentially unchanged attitude. "In my mind, it's always about a very modern cool girl or boy. I'm not afraid to take a risk. My vision is always, 'What is modern?' I still believe in what the whole grunge thing pioneered: ease, effortless dressing," she smiles. "And anyway, when I'm working, I still feel like I'm having fun with my friends."

Opposite:
David Sims
The Face
1990

This page and
opposite:
David Sims
i-D
1993

INSPIRATION

Self-taught Dutch photographer and film-maker Ed van der Elsken was known for his raw, unstyled work. His influence can be seen in the strong graphic lines of Ward's images and her choice of unpretentious subjects, such as in the photograph, opposite, shot by Inez van Lamsweerde and Vinoodh Matadin for *Harper's Bazaar* in 2000.

Opposite:
Inez van Lamsweerde
and Vinoodh Matadin
Harper's Bazaar
2001

This page:
David Sims
Harper's Bazaar
2004

INSPIRATION

The impulse for Ward's collaboration with photographer Patrick Demarchelier for *Harper's Bazaar* in 1999, opposite, was provided by a series of portraits of rock legend Patti Smith, as well as the American sculptor John Chamberlain's *Three-Cornered Desire*, at right. Ward captured Smith's self-assuredness and combined this attitude with the colors and forms of Chamberlain's sculpture into a single pose.

This page and
opposite:
Inez van Lamsweerde
and Vinoodh Matadin
Helmut Lang
advertising campaign
2003

MELANIE WARD

BORN
England

LIVES IN
New York

PHOTOGRAPHERS
Corinne Day, Craig McDean, David Sims, Nick Knight, Nigel Shafran

PUBLICATIONS
Harper's Bazaar

CAMPAIGNS
Calvin Klein

Opposite: Melanie Ward photographed by Inez van Lamsweerde and Vinoodh Matadin for *V*, 2003. This page, clockwise from top left: Ward with hairstylist Kevin Ryan; Ward (at left), with her brother, Anthony, who is now a photographer; Ward's country house.

JOE ZEE

As the fashion director in the hot seat when *W* magazine became a large-format perfect-bound monthly, Joe Zee is one of the stylists who brokered the meeting of fashion, art photography, and celebrity at the turn of the millennium. Commissions from the likes of Philip-Lorca diCorcia, Tina Barney, and Michel Gondry effectively changed the pages into a hybrid of gallery and magazine, a transformation that began to reset the parameters of what was to become possible in fashion imagery.

Once a fashion trade and high-society chronicle, *W*, under Zee's watch, became home to a new genre of sophisticated pop-celebrity photography that helped to change the rules about who should model clothes in rarefied fashion magazines. "Celebrity has become such a huge part of fashion culture that models are now almost obsolete," observes Zee. "This whole interest in the celebrity world has taken over, and it's no longer just the domain of tabloids. I never ran away from that. I like celebrities—they have opinions, careers. I did so many for *W*. I think over time they knew they were coming in for an image overhaul." Zee once lent Britney Spears the weight of a cool comparison to the blonde Velvet Underground icon Nico (though Spears had no idea who the woman was). When Justin Timberlake needed a sharper, more grown-up look for his *FutureSex/LoveSounds* album and tour, Zee was on the case, putting him in sharp Dior Homme tailoring and pieces from the cult Belgian designer Raf Simons; he then arranged for the edgy Terry Richardson to shoot him.

Zee's body of work with art photographers was, he says, partly inspired by movies but mostly by travel. "So many stories started from the cities I was constantly traveling to for work—Bangkok, Amsterdam, Moscow, Paris, São Paulo, Acapulco, Tulsa." That photographers whose prints were already changing hands for hundreds of thousands of dollars would be interested in doing work for a fashion magazine was a credit to Zee's persuasive skills, as well as being given free rein to create their highly staged psychological dramas, which could then roam across extra-large, well-printed glossy pages. "I think it changed people's view of how fashion could be presented. It straddled the line between the tradition of saying, 'this is how a woman should put herself together,' and really telling a story."

Zee's skill as a master of crossover has now taken him into the mainstream, as creative director of *Elle*. "When *Elle* started, in the sixties and seventies, it was about sexy, strong, trendsetting women who would mix things up and look great. I wanted to bring that back." What he took to the job from his tenureship at *W*, he says, is a drive to present fashion in a modern way, reflecting the multiple influences that shape how women dress today. "Women really aren't dictated to just by runways anymore. They take from celebrities, music, movies. They shop high, and they shop low."

If his acute image-making skills make him a very contemporary behind-the-scenes figure, he credits the formation of his eye to the studying he did at high school in Toronto. "I was a kid who sat there with *Vogue* and would look at every credit and name on the masthead, then test myself on them. Later on I realized I loved publishing as much as the photography. The whole package—I loved it all!"

Armed with his schoolboy fashion knowledge, Zee applied to Condé Nast's human resources department in 1992, and immediately landed a job working with Polly Mellen and Lori Goldstein on the then-new *Allure* magazine, where he learned everything from assisting some of the best names in the business. "I knew Polly's pictures and I sought her out. We hit it off. On my very first day at *Allure*, a brand-new model called Kate Moss came up and Polly assigned a new photographer, Steven Klein, to shoot her. It was incredible to see Polly's enthusiasm for the new or different. For me, what makes this job is enthusiasm and excitement. But," he adds, "I still sing the praises of working like a dog."

Opposite:
Juergen Teller
W
1999

Overleaf:
Tina Barney
W
2001

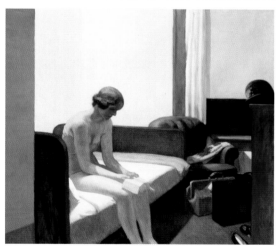

INSPIRATION

American realist Edward Hopper is best known for his paintings depicting the interior life of isolated figures. His masterful use of light and his ability to provoke psychological tension enable his canvases to convey profound statements on the human condition. Above, *Morning Sun*, 1952, and *Hotel Room*, 1931, at left, provided the impulse for Zee's collaboration with artist Philip-Lorca diCorcia, opposite.

This page, opposite,
and overleaf:
Philip-Lorca diCorcia
W
2001

INSPIRATION

Models on repeat and mod pops of bright color in shots from earlier decades find their way into Zee's work with photographer Juergen Teller for *W* magazine in 2002, opposite. Above, photograph by Alberto Rizzo for *Vogue*, 1977; right, photograph by Gosta Peterson for *Vogue*, 1966.

JOE ZEE

BORN
Hong Kong (raised in Canada)

LIVES IN
New York

PHOTOGRAPHERS
Annie Leibovitz, Bruce Weber, Carter Smith, Inez van Lamsweerde and Vinoodh Matadin, Juergen Teller, Mario Sorrenti, Mark Seliger, Matt Jones, Michael Thompson, Mikael Jansson, Patric Shaw, Patrick Demarchelier, Peter Lindbergh, Philip-Lorca diCorcia, Regan Cameron, Richard Avedon, Terry Richardson, Tom Munro

PUBLICATIONS
Allure, Details, Elle, Vanity Fair, Vitals, W

CAMPAIGNS
Anne Klein, Banana Republic, Chanel Cosmetics, Celine, DKNY, Escada, Estée Lauder, Gap, H&M, Jones New York, Kenneth Cole, M.A.C., Maybelline, Oscar de la Renta, Perry Ellis, Sarah Jessica Parker's Lovely, Sean John, Tiffany & Co. Album cover art and packaging for Janet Jackson, Jennifer Lopez, Justin Timberlake, Madonna, Mariah Carey.

Opposite: Joe Zee photographed by Tom Munro for *W*, 2002. This page, top: Zee at work in front of his inspiration wall; bottom: a behind-the-scenes shot of Zee styling dancers from a nightclub in Bangkok for a 2001 *W* shoot.

BRANA WOLF

Designers do not go to Brana Wolf for a soft and pretty point of view. The faces and gestures that jump from her book are strong, direct, and confident—studies in personality that zero in on intelligence and complexity. Wolf's visual world is populated by feisty women rather than unformed girls, and, in so far as the stylist's life is reflected in her work, the woman-of-the-world look of Wolf's pictures is all of a piece with her personal story. A multilingual Australian with Montenegrin ancestry, she worked her way through magazine assignments in Paris and Milan in the eighties, ending up in New York—where she still resides—in the nineties. Along the way, Wolf became a top-flight freelance stylist and design consultant, and a contributing editor for *Harper's Bazaar*. Most people see Wolf as having a modern-classic aesthetic. She likes to bring things down to their barest essentials—real clothes for real women with a sense of modern chic.

When looking at Wolf's advertising work for Dolce & Gabbana and Versace, or her covers for Italian *Vogue*, one might assume that the stylist was Italian: the photographs, which were shot by Steven Meisel, focus on celebrating the power of the sophisticated grown-up—the sort of appreciation natural to Mediterranean cultures. The pictures also come layered with resonances gleaned from the history of cinema and fashion photography. Wolf assisted when Dolce & Gabbana transformed Linda Evangelista into a nineties amalgam of Sophia Loren, Anna Magnani, and Monica Vitti straight out of mid-century neorealist cinema; more recently, she helped channel homages to Helmut Newton and David Bailey into D&G's advertising. Some of Wolf's other favorite stories with Meisel include shoots for Italian *Vogue* based on *Grey Gardens*, the cult documentary about the eccentric, faded grandeur of Edith and Edie Bouvier Beale; *They Shoot Horses, Don't They?*; and research on the graphics of the Bauhaus.

To be fluent and knowledgeable about the visual meaning of all these sources is a vital part of a stylist's job, but it's equally important to avoid suffocating the fashion message with such references. Wolf's down-to-earth antipodean pragmatism strikes that balance. For her, an imaginative shoot that alludes to links between current fashion and movies or art should still be anchored in clothes women will want to own. "My favorite clothes in any season are the wearable ones," she shrugs. "The things that make me excited are always the pieces I could put on myself. I care about cut and quality and shape and fabric, not the loud stuff." The result she aims for is essentially "expensive good taste."

Wolf's expertise, formidable organizational bent, and capacity for straight talking mean that her opinions have value. Over the past decade, as the power of the industry has boomed and the need for coherent global marketing imagery has become ever more important to fashion brands, she has frequently been tapped by designers as a consultant. This behind-the-scenes designer-stylist relationship can shade into many levels of involvement with a collection, from advising on trends to contributing design ideas, attending fittings, casting models, organizing shows, and completing advertising campaigns. Designers would invite her up to have a look at the clothes before the show and ask for her opinion, and it started from there. With Michael Kors she simply acts as "a sounding board" and backstage coordinator, while with Donatella Versace she starts at sketch and fabric selection, suggesting to "shorten this, or add that."

As an outside eye who also travels freely through other designers' houses, seeing clothes and choosing pieces for her editorial shoots, Wolf—and all the others like her in the complex political network of stylist/designer relationships—is in a position of trust and confidence that cannot be violated. She maintains an extremely professional outlook, and avoids crossovers between the different things she does. When asked why she is still sought out by magazines and designers more than twenty-five years since her first job as a beauty department fact-checker for *Jasmine Magazine* in Sydney, Wolf laughs. "I think I'm an old-school type, in that I can do very edgy, and I can do commercial. And I never felt it was about me—it's always about the project."

Opposite and
overleaf:
Inez van Lamsweerde
and Vinoodh Matadin
Harper's Bazaar
2000

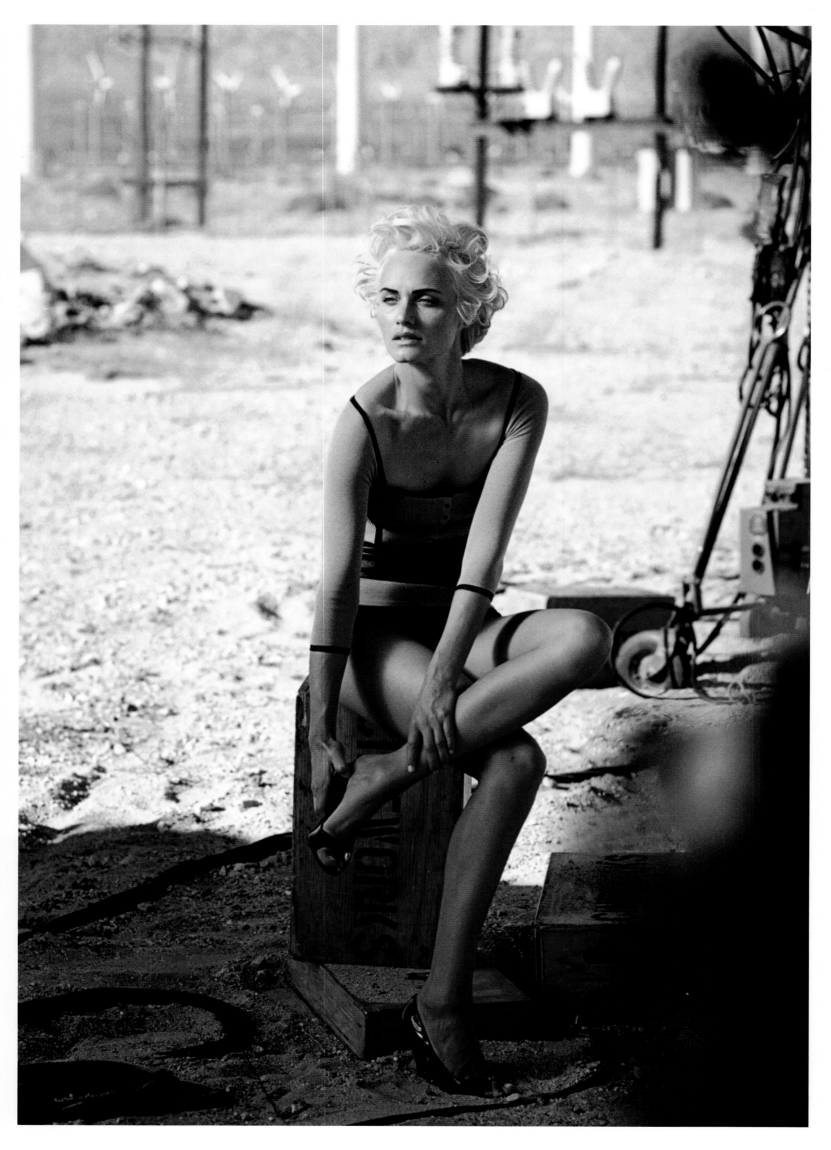

Pages 130–31   This page and
Steven Meisel   opposite:
Dolce & Gabbana   Peter Lindbergh
advertising campaign *Harper's Bazaar*
2006   2003

This page:
Steven Meisel
Italian *Vogue*
2006

Opposite:
Inez van Lamsweerde
and Vinoodh Matadin
Louis Vuitton
advertising campaign
2000

Overleaf:
Tony Viramontes
Italian *Vogue*
1997

BRANA WOLF

BORN
Italy (raised in Australia)

LIVES IN
New York

PHOTOGRAPHERS
Inez van Lamsweerde and Vinoodh Matadin,
Mario Sorrenti, Nathaniel Goldberg, Patrick Demarchelier,
Peter Lindbergh, Steven Meisel, Terry Tsolis

PUBLICATIONS
Harper's Bazaar, Italian Vogue

CAMPAIGNS
Brioni, Dolce & Gabbana, Ferragamo, Valentino, Versace

Opposite: Brana Wolf
photographed by Inez
van Lamsweerde and
Vinoodh Matadin for *V*.
This page, clockwise
from top: Brana with
models Amber Valletta
and Nadja Auermann;
Brana with hairstylist
Sam McKnight; on set
with Linda Evangelista;
Brana on location
in Kenya.

ANDREA LIEBERMAN

Andrea Lieberman epitomizes the ascendance of the music-business stylist. She belongs to a new breed of creative connectors at the forefront of the instant communication age—image brokers who have been responsible for binding together celebrity, high fashion, and street culture into an unstoppable force. "I run an image-production company," she says. "My method is to create an image for an artist that ends up being a tool for marketing—from record to video to tour to Web site." The fact that Lieberman is speaking during a break from her current job, an

Estée Lauder advertising shoot in the south of France for Sean "Diddy" Combs's new fragrance, also attests to the extent that music-world talent has permeated the center of fashion power, in front of the camera and behind it.

Lieberman started working with Diddy and his then-girlfriend Jennifer Lopez "when they were just blowing up," she recalls. "I was smack in the middle of it." She was the person who put Lopez in a plunging jungle-print Versace gown for the 2000 Grammy Awards, a "moment" that could be designated as the exact point when, in a giant flash of paparazzi attention, high fashion and young celebrity fused into the white-hot phenomenon of the new millennium. Still, it is not Lopez but Gwen Stefani who is Lieberman's most consistently unmissable client. With the release of each successive video, Stefani's high-color mishmashed fantasias of all-American glam and sportswear have had a major influence on young fashion. "Gwen is just this unbelievable, stunning, iconic woman," says Lieberman. "We've grown up together. I became an editor to her. The artist I'm working with becomes my muse; I become the eyes and ears."

In Stefani's videos, she and Lieberman have made a series of fashion epics smashed into three minutes of constant costume changes and multiple clashes of clothes. "Rich Girl" mixed Rasta hats and sweats, eighteenth-century pirate gear, twenties lingerie, and more. "What You Waiting For?" went on an Alice-in-Wonderland trip involving top hats, frayed denim hot pants, white stockings, corsets, and Christian Dior haute couture gowns and crowns. In "Hollaback Girl," Stefani's gang of bad girls romped through an outrageous raid on cheerleader wardrobe. Of course, all these were threaded through with cartwheeling appearances from the Harajuku Girls, the dancing Japanese pop-kitsch cuties that appear in many of Stefani's promos and live performances.

Lieberman describes what she does in terms of "layers" of inspiration, comparing her methods to those used by the musicians she works with. "It's all about the remix. You might take the tune from one place, the beat from somewhere else, but then put in a bridge of your own—that would be me getting a piece of jewelry." The result is busy and maximal but, paradoxically, it has proved so accessible that its influence has been assimilated by teen fans

without a hiccup. In 2003, when Stefani launched her own line, L.A.M.B., it was natural that she should rely on Lieberman to translate the clothes from costume to salable reality. Thus the music-stylist-turned-designer; which, as it turns out, is exactly how Lieberman was trained in the first place.

Lieberman's ability to orchestrate her decade- and culture-dipping extravaganzas is based on a vivid stockpile of visual memories, travel experiences, and a solid grounding in fashion from Parsons School of Design. As a blue-Mohawked teenager, she spent hours in the New York Public Library "getting lost in old copies of *Vogue*," and "fogging up the windows" of the Matsuda and Kenzo stores. After graduating with a bachelor's degree in 1992, she took off for Africa for two years. "It all clicked for me there," she says. "I really felt inspired by the rituals and the cultural meaning of dressing and adornment." Lieberman also picked up a passion for jewelry, returning to New York to sell pieces she'd bought on her travels, then falling into styling young actresses for *Time Out New York* magazine covers and helping a photographer who was making videos for aspiring young bands.

An assignment styling Diddy for *Vibe* magazine began one of the long-lasting relationships that has propelled Lieberman's career constantly upward. Still, she claims, "I'm sort of self-trained. In the beginning, designers wouldn't lend clothes to pop people, so it was all about going into costume hire shops." A decade later, the system has changed so drastically that designers now beg to be involved with the sort of work Lieberman produces. That's nice, but having the whole world of official fashion eating out of her hand is never going to completely satisfy Lieberman's eclectic roving eye. "I'm constantly searching for inspiration, adding another layer. For example, I'll be in Jamaica, and I'll pass an off-the-wall guy wearing a V-neck pink sweater, Adidas sweats, and a giant tam, and it somehow ends up in a video. That," she concludes, "is what drives me."

Opposite:
Nick Knight
Album art for
Gwen Stefani's
*Love. Angel.
Music. Baby.*
2004

Opposite:
"What You Waiting
For?" music video

Francis Lawrence,
director
2004

This page:
Mert Alas and
Marcus Piggott
Coty Prestige

advertisement for
L, a L.A.M.B. fragrance
by Gwen Stefani
2007

INSPIRATION

For Gwen Stefani's music video "Luxurious," opposite, Lieberman's palette was influenced by the vibrant colors, piles of jewelry, and chicified ethnic aesthetic worn by model Veruschka in one of Franco Rubartelli's 1968 shoots for *Vogue*, below and at right.

INSPIRATION

Lieberman's work with photographer Mark Squires for his 2005 portrait of Gwen Stefani appearing in *Complex*, opposite, drew from a pool of images, such as Diego Rivera's photograph of Frida Kahlo and Emmy Lou Packard, a painter, printmaker, and muralist who once lived with the couple as assistant to Rivera. Lieberman also took cues from Nickolas Muray's portrait of Kahlo, bottom left, held in the George Eastman House collection, and Franco Rubartelli's photograph of a wrapped Veruschka, in 1968, from the pages of *Vogue*. The influence of simple yet striking Mexican peasant dresses, worn by both Kahlo and Packard, and the idea of wrapping and adorning both hair and bodice and combining different textures all contributed to Lieberman's vision.

This page:
Michel Comte
Italian *Vogue*
2004

Opposite:
Annie Leibovitz
Vanity Fair
1998

Overleaf:
"Cool" music video
Sophie Muller,
director
2004

ANDREA LIEBERMAN

BORN
United States

LIVES IN
New York

PHOTOGRAPHERS
Albert Watson, Annie Leibovitz, David LaChapelle, Gilles Bensimon, Glen Luchford, Herb Ritz, James White, Lorenzo Agius, Marc Baptiste, Marc Hom, Mark Liddell, Mark Seliger, Mark Squires, Markus Klinko, Martin Schoeller, Matt Jones, Matthew Rolston, Max Vadukul, Mert Alas and Marcus Piggott, Michel Comte, Nick Knight, Norman Jean Roy, Patrick Demarchelier, Peter Lindbergh, Richard Phibbs, Ruven Afanador, Tony Duran

PUBLICATIONS
Allure, Arena, Blender, British Vogue, Complex, Elle, Elle UK, Esquire, Glamour, GQ, Harpers & Queen, Harper's Bazaar, i-D, InStyle, Italian Vogue, Marie Claire, Nylon, Paper, People, Rolling Stone, Seventeen, British Sunday Times, Teen People, Teen Vogue, Trace, Vanity Fair, VIBE

CAMPAIGNS
Chevrolet, Diet Coke, Estée Lauder Unforgivable, Glow, Got Milk, Hanes, Jette Joop, JLo, L.A.M.B., Lux, Martell, Panasonic D-3-o, Skyy Vodka, Still, Subaru. Album cover art and packaging for Faith Hill's *Cry*, Gwen Stefani's *Love.Angel.Music.Baby.* and *The Sweet Escape*, Janet Jackson's *20 Y.O.*, Jennifer Lopez's *This Is Me . . . Then*, Mary J. Blige's *The Breakthrough*.

Opposite:
Andrea Lieberman, photographed by James White. This page, top: Andrea as a child; middle: Andrea on location, researching; bottom, left: the stylist sampling fabrics; bottom, right: Andrea styling Gwen Stefani.

PAUL CAVACO

It's hopeless to adopt an awestruck voice when talking to Paul Cavaco. "I'm from the ghetto. I'm lower-middle class. I don't understand 'fancy,'" he will insist. "But I get New York." This typically offhand self-portrait belies the fact that Cavaco, the creative director of *Allure*, occupies a permanent place of respect in the upper reaches of American fashion. His reputation stretches back through tenureships at *Vogue* and *Harper's Bazaar* in the 1990s, to the inception of Keeble, Cavaco & Duka, the agency that laid down the template for modern standards in fashion public relations in the 1980s.

Cavaco's portfolio has a breadth and diversity that spans luminously intimate beauty photographs, elegant fashion stories, and large-scale location productions involving dozens of people. "Do I have a style? Probably not," he shrugs. "I'm usually trying to be the personality of the photographer. I have to channel who they are, even if I came up with the idea." Equally reputed for his aesthetic rigor and pomposity-puncturing sense of humor, Cavaco's personality creates a force field into which people are drawn to do their best. Even though his shoots famously rock with laughter, he takes the business of producing fashion imagery far more seriously than he will admit. "I like the collaborative process. I don't mind being second, third, or fourth," he says. "If I believe in the photographer, I can align right behind them."

Cavaco credits the beginning of his career to his late ex-wife, the fashion editor Kezia Keeble, and the fact that, in the late seventies, they were broke. "I was a waiter at the Brew Burger on 57th and 5th—all the beer you could drink!—and Kezia was pregnant. Sometimes I'd be on nightshift, so I'd go on shoots to help her." Keeble, who had worked for Diana Vreeland at *Vogue* and had been an editor at *Glamour* in the sixties, was one of the first to go freelance in the seventies. Cavaco first glimpsed her world when she recommended he go for a casting at *Esquire*. "They were doing a college issue. I'd just graduated school and I became one of the five models. All the guys were six feet and taller, except for me; short, with a big nose and glasses. The foil. The doofus." The photographer was Bruce Weber, who liked Cavaco's clothes sense so much he hired him to style a DAKS ad.

Thus, husband and wife effectively became a freelance fashion family business, crossing between editorial and advertising work in a way that eventually bumped up the professional status of the stylist. Among Cavaco's best-known shoots were Calvin Klein's first Obsession ad; the "three Diors" campaign with Richard Avedon; and Nair ads with Bill King, which featured the then young teen models, Whitney Houston and Phoebe Cates. He also did dozens of assignments for *Vogue*, Italian *Vogue*, *GQ*, *Esquire*, *Per Lui*, and *Lei*.

Until Cavaco and his wife arrived, magazines credited only the photographer, and hair and makeup people. "Kezia asked, 'Why not get credit? We're part of this,'" he says. "So the first time there was a styling credit in a magazine, it read 'Produced by Keeble Cavaco.' Also, we needed our names out there." Mentored by Keeble, Cavaco developed a deliberately "invisible" touch, choosing and tweaking clothes so they looked like they belonged to the model—the revolutionary early eighties aesthetic pioneered in Bruce Weber's naturalistic photography. "What Bruce was doing was brand-new. It was that changing point, coming off seventies disco, with clothes that were a little easier, with a beautiful realism. The models in his shots were stripped down, without much makeup, and every picture was pumped with light. Bruce's whole thing would be, 'Don't be shy! Put those crazy colors together!' So we did a lot of weird, crazy things; I'd take the sleeves off jackets, mix in a lot of vintage."

One day, Frances Grill, a legendary photographers' agent, met with Keeble and Cavaco over a carousel of test shots by an aspiring photographer. "Kezia and I projected his pictures onto the back of our front door." It was an immediate click. The photos were Steven Meisel's. "We're about the same age—Steven and I—same sensibility, same socioeconomic background; we're New Yorkers. We don't mind the streets." Working with Meisel crystallized Cavaco's vision of what fashion could be. "I'm not 'to the manor born,' which was a big thing in fashion in the seventies. Kezia would always say, 'Try to be true in a picture. You can see it in people's photographs if they're not being honest.'" Part of the culture Cavaco shared with Meisel and Weber was an addiction to cinema. "All I did was watch movies when I was a kid, so Meisel could refer to the way Faye Dunaway looked in *Bonnie and Clyde* and I'd get it. I have a visual movie vocabulary."

In spite of the way he downplays his talent, Cavaco analyzes every image with razor-sharp precision. "Richard Avedon would ask, 'What's the surprise?' And you'd go, 'It's the purple sock,' so he'd go 'Okay, move the pant leg up.' I worked with great visual people who would ask, 'Why am I looking at this? What is great about this girl? Yes, she's beautiful, but they're all beautiful. Show me what is different. Is it lipstick; is it not? What is that hand doing? Is it just shoved in the pocket? Should it be out or should it be showing a nail?' You have all these options; what are you going to choose? The world is that open; how do you make it yours? That's the editing process."

Most of all, though, the central link between Cavaco's pictures is the alternately elegiac, satirical, romantic, hilarious, and chic imagery of New York that surfaces over and again. "I love living here—the way it looks when it's pretty and when it's dirty," he says. "Things I know, that I can understand." Ultimately, though, Cavaco never claims credit for any image created under his watch. "When I look at something, I think, 'I didn't actually do this, but, in my space, the possibility was there for something great to happen.'"

Opposite:
Steven Meisel
Italian *Vogue*
1991

VOGUE

ITALIA

MAG.
1991
N. 489
L. 6.000

Estate
in spiaggia:
ginnastica
diete sole

ABITI
CHIC E
PREZIOSI

ABITO PRADA

IL RITORNO DEL
BIANCO:
JEANS BODY
COSTUME

INSPIRATION

The black-and-white photograph from *Harper's Bazaar*, right, was a point of departure for Cavaco's collaboration with photographer Steven Meisel on the cover of Italian *Vogue's* May 1991 issue, left, co-styled by Anna Sui, was Erwin Blumenfeld's legendary 1950 cover for *Vogue*, featuring Jean Patchett's minimal profile. The full red lips, smoky eye, immaculate brow, and beauty mark represent the essence of glamour.

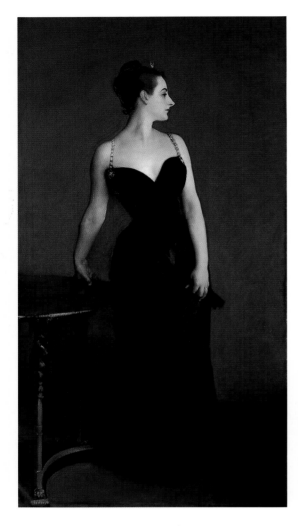

INSPIRATION

Scandalous when it hit the art scene in 1884, John Singer Sargent's iconic *Madame X*, left, was the impulse for Cavaco's reinterpretation of the famous portrait with Nicole Kidman in the starring role, opposite, photographed by Steven Meisel for *Vogue* in 1999. A similar influence was one of Sargent's watercolor and graphite studies of Madame Gautreau, below.

Pages 158–59:   This page: Opposite:
Michael Thompson   Peter Lindbergh   David Sims
Allure   *Harper's Bazaar*   *Harper's Bazaar*
2002   1992   1993

Opposite: This page: Overleaf:
Bruce Weber   Steven Meisel   Bruce Weber
SoHo Weekly News *Rolling Stone*   *Per Lui*
1978   1991   1985

PAUL CAVACO

BORN
United States

LIVES IN
New York

PHOTOGRAPHERS
Bill King, Bruce Weber, Mario Testino, Michael Thompson, Patrick Demarchelier, Richard Avedon, Steven Meisel

PUBLICATIONS
Allure, GQ, Harper's Bazaar, Interview, Italian Vogue, Lei, Per Lui, Vogue

CAMPAIGNS
Calvin Klein, Calvin Klein Obsession, Dior, Dolce & Gabbana, Nair, Prada, Valentino

Opposite: Paul Cavaco and Christy Turlington, photographed by Steven Meisel. This page, clockwise from top left: Julien d'Ys, Kevin Aucoin, Paul Cavaco, and Kim Williams, photographed by Steven Meisel after a Geoffrey Beene advertising campaign shoot; Cavaco, photographed by Bruce Weber in the late '70s/early '80s, after a shoot in Bellport, Long Island; Cavaco styling a model on set; a signed Bruce Weber photograph, which was taken following a shoot for the *SoHo Weekly News* in New Jersey's Seaside Heights, 1978.

VENETIA SCOTT

The term stylist is so diffuse, it can cover almost as many ways of working as there are people who get paid to dress models, actors, politicians, and celebrities. The elusive British Venetia Scott stretches the definition further. In the nineteenth century she would have been labeled an artist's muse—the idea certainly fits the slant of her Pre-Raphaelite ruralist looks. While that comparison partly captures the intensity of her behind-the-scenes relationships, however, Scott's contributions have an effectiveness beyond that of any eccentric "spirit" in the studio. Since 1997 Scott has been a central member of Marc Jacobs's close-knit design team. Her stamp—downplayed vintage college-kid style drawn from personal memories and 1970s thrift-shop leftovers—is particularly visible in the Marc by Marc Jacobs line, of which she serves as creative director. Silent her input may be, but anyone who has purchased a coat with big plastic buttons, a military jacket, or high-rise jeans copied from Jacobs has unwittingly fallen for her taste.

Scott also helped foment the deeper shift in aesthetics that washed over fashion in the early nineties. Once aptly described by the art director Phil Bicker as a "stylist of understatement," she says, simply, "I always want you to see the girl, and then have the clothes tell you something more about her." During the late eighties it was Scott's uncompromising perception of an alternative, unretouched beauty that pushed her then-boyfriend Juergen Teller into the controversially raw style of photography that made his name. Their anti-fashion, radically naturalistic shoots were, as Teller put it, about "scraping things down." The subversive impact of their sideways-on narratives was to make a perfect paradigm of the contradictory, assimilating mechanism of fashion. By the late nineties, the dissenting outsiders had infiltrated the center of the system, Teller's work was being sought after by art collectors, and Scott was hired as a right-hand creative consultant by Jacobs—about as high as a stylist could go.

Scott met Teller when she was at loose ends after a four-year stint at British *Vogue*. Assisting the fashion editors Sophie Hicks and Grace Coddington on the magazine she witnessed the late-eighties rise of glamazonian power dressing and was permanently awestruck by the frisson of English correctness—"a sort of discipline and perfection" pervasive in *Vogue*'s central London headquarters. Finding herself jobless at twenty-four, however, the rebel in Scott—which had been present since her days as a recidivist runaway from English boarding school—took over. Styling for Perry Ogden and Michel Haddi, who used "real" extras in semi-documentary fashion shoots, had made her start to think differently about photography and casting. "And then I met Juergen, who fully got it," she says.

Together they captured young faces in road stories and country landscapes that narrowed the distinction between fashion and reportage almost to the vanishing point. "It was a reaction against being at *Vogue* and all the things I was impressed by," she says. "It was about going to festivals, being back in jeans and Birkenstocks—at ease instead of in Alaïa." Partly, too, the work was inspired by Scott's shock of recognition when she first saw Larry Clark's *Teenage Lust*, and a photograph by Joseph Szabo of a long-haired hoyden, no more than thirteen years old, on a beach and smoking a cigarette. "I loved the feeling of freedom and vitality, that they were fearless; the opposite of what I felt at school."

When Scott gathered thrift-shop clothes to mix with current fashion, they were autobiographical resurrections of the kinds of things her mother and hippy big sister wore in the seventies while living a nomadic army-family life in the Middle East. Those themes recur in her work with Jacobs, and, since she split with Teller, in the photographs she has started to take. "I was the one who would often have the idea. I've become tired of handing over those ideas to photographers who then get the credit."

Today, living in London's Notting Hill, Scott is as unconventional and contradictory as ever, workspace tackboards betraying the dichotomy that runs through her stories. Alongside printouts of fashion shows hang photos of a renegade traveler community's encampment of tents, huts, and trucks buried somewhere deep in England's West Country; it's a prospective location for an *Another Magazine* shoot. "Half of me wants to go and live with them. And the other half is more this"—she points to an incendiary photograph of a woman dressed only in high heels, underpants, and a mask, standing in a luxurious contemporary house in the California sunshine. The link between the wildly lawless teenager and the powerfully sexual grown-up woman is, she insists, inherent to the characters in the pictures, both ideal projections of her fantasy selves. "I really don't think like other stylists. It's not about the fashion," she insists. "It's about a dream girl."

Opposite:
Juergen Teller
Katharine Hamnett
advertising campaign
1997

Opposite:
David Sims
The Face
1993

This page:
Juergen Teller
The Face
1996

INSPIRATION

Joseph Szabo's image of a windswept girl with a hand to her forehead is at once stark and intimate. Scott's work reflects this idea of drawing the viewer into a private moment while reminding them that they are, ultimately, voyeurs.

Larry Clark's candid and provocative black-and-white shots of youths on the edge embody an effortless attitude which Scott channeled in her work with Juergen Teller for *The Face* in 1996, opposite.

This page:
Juergen Teller
Italian *Vogue*
1996

Opposite:
Juergen Teller
Nova

INSPIRATION

Scott discovered Joseph Szabo's out-of-focus black-and-white images of children and teens years after her collaboration, in 1990, with Juergen Teller for *i-D*, opposite, but felt a sense of artistic empathy with the photographer. She continues to turn to his work today, finding inspiration in his portrayals of teenage rebellion.

This page:
Marc Jacobs, fall
2005 ready-to-wear.
Photography by
Marcio Madeira/
Style.com

Opposite:
Marc Jacobs
advertising campaign
2003

VENETIA SCOTT

BORN
England

LIVES IN
London

PHOTOGRAPHERS
David Sims, Helmut Newton, Juergen Teller,
Mario Sorrenti, Stephen Shore

PUBLICATIONS
Another Magazine, i-D, Italian Vogue, Nova, Self Service, W

CAMPAIGNS
Calvin Klein Eternity, CK Jeans, Katharine Hamnett,
Marc Jacobs, Margaret Howell

Opposite: Venetia Scott
and her daughter, Lola,
photographed by
Juergen Teller for *Self
Service*, 2002. This
page, clockwise from
top left: Scott as a child
in Iran with her family;
Scott photographed by
her father, John Scott,
in 1972; Scott with
Lola, photographed by
Teller; Scott on set.

TONNE GOODMAN

If the United States were scoured for one person who best embodies pared-down American style, the search might well end with Tonne Goodman. Her inimitable reductive touch is capable of turning something as ordinary as a plain white shirt into such an object of rightness and restraint that it seems to summon the best of American ideals. "I am very austere and very American," Goodman says. "But it's not only that I like austere clothes. It's the sensibility that you apply to everything. I like things clean as a whistle. Reaching the decision of what to use is always thorough, to the bone. I like it when a buttonhole has been given the same grace as the embroidery. It sounds pretentious, but when you find that, there's a level of honesty there."

Tall, fine-boned, and rangy, Goodman has moved through the New York fashion industry since she first stepped into a studio as a teenage model in the early seventies, after which she went on to become vice president for advertising at Calvin Klein and fashion director at *Harper's Bazaar* in the mid-nineties. Her eye was honed by working for two giant personalities of the New York press, Diana Vreeland and Carrie Donovan, fashion editor of the *New York Times* magazine. Now fashion director at *Vogue*, Goodman is the hand behind many celebrity covers and practically every story that calls for a crisp edit to bring clarity to an indistinct season.

Goodman's scrupulously principled tastes were formed, of course, as a girl. "You get it from what you're exposed to as a child, and I was exposed to an enormously elegant mother, and a father who was—if possible—even more elegant," she says. Edmund Goodman was a surgeon who served in the navy ("with the looks of Gregory Peck," according to his daughter); Marian, his wife, was a textile designer from Ohio who reveled in taking her children to every museum, gallery, and theater in New York. Tonne was sent to The Brearley School, where she acquired her lifelong tic of correct, clean, simple dressing, before studying art in Italy. "It's a New York private-girls'-school style," she laughs. "It comes back to haunt you."

If it can be defined, Goodman's look is the unshowy refinement of New England and the Upper East Side: an innate knowledge of how to put things together—a home, as much as an outfit—with an economy of elements of the highest quality. If references come into her imagery, they will often relate to her interest in modern American art and architecture (evident in her love of stark gallery spaces and mid-century landmarks as locations); echo her student days in the painting studio; or, with an almost undetectable subtlety, channel her heroines—great American women of style and substance like Slim Keith, Katharine Hepburn, Lee Miller, and the designer Claire McCardell. And if dispensing with superfluous clutter is the essence of Goodman's discipline with clothes, that applies just as much to her arrow-straight vision of the point of her work. "I am a feminist. I believe in women," she declares. "My work is ultimately about a strong woman. It's not frilly; it's about honesty and conviction. In the end, that strength is probably the greatest elegance."

An early version of Goodman's style is immortalized in a favorite souvenir of her modeling days, a 1971 sportswear shoot by Irving Penn in *Vogue*, in which she posed in golf and tennis clothes next to a Gucci caddy. She looks uncannily like Christy Turlington who, during Goodman's time at Calvin Klein and later during her editorship at *Harper's Bazaar*, became a favorite subject in her work—styled, of course, as the thoroughbred American natural. Twenty years later, in 2002, Goodman and Steven Meisel amused themselves by revisiting the Penn shot for a "Palm Beach woman" versus a "St. Bart's woman" sportswear story—this time with Carmen Kass and a caddy from Louis Vuitton in the frame.

Goodman started modeling during her tenth grade summer holiday, when, as a fashion-crazed teen, she briefly worked for *Mademoiselle*. She remembers having "an asymmetric Sassoon cut, the shortest damn skirts, and long skinny legs." After studying at Philadelphia School of Art, Goodman was again scouted on the street in New York, this time by a *Vogue* fashion editor. "Kezia Keeble found me on the sidewalk in a blue shift-dress with vast black-and-white platform mules. She took me up to see Mrs. Vreeland. I would come in for run-throughs in her office and she used me twice as a model, so mine wasn't a massive career by any means. But I learned so much from watching Mrs. Vreeland. She was a sharpshooter. She knew what she wanted. That was my first exposure to an editor in the studio and in the office."

After a year studying art in Perugia, Italy, Goodman returned to New York and ended up with Vreeland again. "She was starting to mount exhibitions at the Costume Institute at the Met. I was called her 'special assistant.' I'd walk around the gallery taking notes on what she wanted. She taught me, point-blank, always ask the question. There's nothing wrong with not knowing. And talk only to the top. Pretty good lessons." Then she went to work at the *New York Times* magazine for Carrie Donovan. "It was weekly, and you did everything. Called in clothes, did the credits, wrote the copy. You can do anything after that."

Opposite:
Steven Meisel
Vogue
2005

Overleaf:
Steven Meisel
Vogue
2003

This page: Opposite:
Steven Klein   Craig McDean
Vogue   *Vogue*
2002   2007

This page and
opposite:
Bruce Weber
Calvin Klein
advertising campaign
1988–89

This page:
Peter Lindbergh
Harper's Bazaar
1994

Opposite:
One of Tonne
Goodman's personal
collages.

TO MOMMK FOR MEVIE

KODAK 5063 TX 23A → 24
KODAK 5063 TX 24A → 30
25 31

MRS. VREELAND   Date Monday, 2 November, 70

nt:

ONNE GOODMAN

nk Tonne has the makings of a good
— strength and ease in getting
he ground."

has not learned how to smile or
her eyes or to make herself extra-
ry with her face.

s something you must teach a model
en see to it that she carries it out!

do not fail with this girl - though
not pretty - she pulls together
bones and proportion in an aristo-
e manner.

See pictures

Opposite:
Irving Penn
Vogue
1971

This page:
Steven Meisel
Vogue
2002

TONNE GOODMAN

BORN
United States

LIVES IN
New York

PHOTOGRAPHERS
Annie Leibovitz, Arthur Elgort, Craig McDean, Helmut Newton, Herb Ritts, Mario Testino, Patrick Demarchelier, Richard Avedon, Steven Klein, Steven Meisel

PUBLICATIONS
Harper's Bazaar, LIFE, New York Times magazine, Self, Vogue

CAMPAIGNS
Anne Klein, Calvin Klein

Opposite: Tonne Goodman photographed by Nicholas Vreeland for *Vogue*, 2005. This page, top: Goodman on set; middle: Goodman photographed for *Vogue*, 2005; bottom left: Goodman and her children; bottom right: Goodman at home photographed by Bruce Weber for *Vogue*, 2001.

LORI GOLDSTEIN

If a project cries out for excess, eccentricity, and a kaleidoscopic explosion of clothes, Lori Goldstein is the stylist to call. "I love layering, different textures, and color. When I'm working for a magazine and they have difficult clothes that they want to fit into a story, I like the challenge. I always get given the tricky clothes, because I can make them look great. My style is definitely a little insane. A mix and match of things that don't go together, but, in the end, do." During times when the fashion cycle has been on the point of swinging from sobriety to flamboyance,

her hand has often been there, giving a crucial nudge. The glossy fall 2000 Versace advertising campaign, created in collaboration with photographer Steven Meisel, was the visual tipping point for the fin-de-millennium moment when fashion went overboard into high-spending logomania. Goldstein's other editorial stories have contributed to the general shift toward a focus on the style of Hollywood teenagers; or they have brought individualistic, thrift-shop dressing to the fore as a fully assimilated, officially recognized fashion of the times.

Goldstein's brand of highly colored eclecticism has an American, specifically West Coast, cast—a perspective imprinted on her as a child of the sixties who moved with her family from Ohio to L.A. "I was just obsessed with fashion," she declares. "I loved color, fun things to wear. My mom married a man who was a cashmere sweater salesman. I loved it. I dreamed about fashion." That girlhood playfulness—Goldstein's sheer joy in clothes—has stayed with her for life. "When I grew up, I could not conform. Even now I can't stand it when things match," she says. "I love mixing color and pattern. There has to be an element of color, a ruffle."

Goldstein got her first job working in L.A. as a sales assistant at Fred Segal in the early seventies, when it was a glam-rock mecca. She remembers selling skintight bell-bottoms, satin baseball jackets—all the rock-star finery. Within three months owner Fred Segal had noticed Goldstein's talent and was taking her on buying trips. "In '78 I came to New York for the first time. I saw the skyline and died. I knew it was where I had to be." Goldstein took a job at Fiorucci—"Where a kid called Marc Jacobs used to come in all the time"—danced at Studio 54 and then the Mudd Club. She began working on her own as a designer's agent, crossing the Atlantic to bring back Vivienne Westwood's wild collections from her World's End shop in London.

In the early eighties, the job spec of a "stylist"—a freelancer, as opposed to a fashion editor employed by a magazine—was yet to be invented. Goldstein was one of those who pioneered the field, which steadily attracted advertising dollars and status as the fashion industry, propelled by the economic boom, began to realize the value of the expert image-maker. "I feel like I've paved the way; 'stylist' used to be a dirty word," says Goldstein. She fell into the job through a hairdresser friend who suggested she help a photographer style some new model "tests." She began working more steadily, and discovered that, at $350 a day, it paid better than her day job. It soon became a regular gig.

By the nineties, Goldstein was working internationally as one of the fashion industry's most respected insiders, forming close bonds with photographer Annie Leibovitz, with whom she worked on American Express campaigns and *Vanity Fair* editorials, and Steven Meisel, undertaking epic Italian *Vogue* editorials and Versace advertising with him. "With Annie, I really learned about a different kind of styling—to make it part of the photography." Meisel's shoots, however, were all about the clothes. "We were doing sixty-page stories for Italian *Vogue* all of a sudden. It was wild. Steven loves fashion. I love shopping for clothes: getting, doing, having . . . all three! That's the fun for me."

Goldstein's favorite stories are the ones that give her eclectic instincts full rein—and those where the fashion is bound up with some kind of social commentary. The Versace campaign that caused such a stir in 2000 portrayed models Amber Valletta and Georgina Grenville as characters from Jacqueline Susann's *Valley of the Dolls*—right down to the big lacquered hair, seventies jet-set clothes, and palatial Beverly Hills interiors. "I was always obsessed with Jacqueline Susann. Steven had just moved to L.A.; it was the beginning of the excess time in fashion, and we thought, 'This is it!' I am a big fan of humor. I look at life, and fashion, that way." After the campaign, Goldstein's rapport with Donatella Versace extended into a consulting role, where she advised on the look of the collection as well as styling the runway show.

Around the same time, after long years of strict minimalism in which richness, decoration, and sensuality had virtually disappeared from fashion pages, Goldstein and Meisel shot a taboo-breaking story on the new buxom model Sophie Dahl, which went overboard in the opposite direction. "I got literally every piece I could from Fred Leighton and put them on her. We had been so devoid of jewelry, diamonds, and sexiness until then."

According to Goldstein, one of the most influential shoots she did with Meisel took place when the pair turned their sights on Hollywood teen culture in 1995; the story held up a mirror to a phenomenon that went on to fuel a tabloid industry. Goldstein put together each outfit as a mishmashed cacophony of kitsch accessories, sportswear and patchworks, jeans and evening pieces, western and punk, fifties and seventies; all were convincingly thrown together with a disregard for correctness that could only be perpetrated by an L.A. kid. It was an anti-style that has since become a style. "I looked back recently," Goldstein says, laughing, "and thought: Mary-Kate and Ashley should really thank us for that!" Those kinds of girl-minded stories are, perhaps, what Goldstein is happiest doing.

Opposite:
Yelena Yemchuk
Japanese *Vogue*
2003

Overleaf:
Mario Sorrenti
W
2005

This page and
opposite:
Steven Meisel
Italian *Vogue*
2000

Opposite:
Yelena Yemchuk
Japanese *Vogue*
2003

This page:
Versace, spring 2000.
Photography by
JB Villareal/
Style.com

Overleaf:
Steven Meisel
Italian *Vogue*
2000

LORI GOLDSTEIN

BORN
United States

LIVES IN
New York

PHOTOGRAPHERS
Annie Leibovitz, Bruce Weber, Glen Luchford, Mario Sorrenti, Mario Testino, Richard Avedon, Steven Meisel, Yelena Yemchuk

PUBLICATIONS
Allure, Italian Vogue, Vanity Fair, W

CAMPAIGNS
American Express, Gap, Harry Winston, Hermès, Prada, Versace

Opposite: Lori Goldstein photographed by Inez van Lamsweerde and Vinoodh Matadin for *V*, 2003. This page, clockwise from top left: Lori's print collection, photographed by William Abranowicz for *Elle Decor*, 2004; Lori in her office, photographed by Minori Yoshida for Japanese *Vogue*, 2003; Lori's living room, photographed by William Abranowicz for *Elle Decor*, 2004; two shots of Lori Goldstein behind the scenes, photographed by Minori Yoshida for Japanese *Vogue*, 2003.

EDWARD ENNINFUL

The remarkable span of Edward Enninful's work—from customizing army surplus to picking out the cream of haute couture—reflects the extreme trajectory of his climb from London's Ladbroke Grove to New York, where he became a *Vogue* contributing editor in 2005. This groundbreaking talent was discovered by *i-D* magazine in London where, aged eighteen, editor-in-chief Terry Jones appointed him fashion director. Cooking up incendiary covers with a cohort of equally gifted and penniless beginners, Enninful's vision propelled the magazine out of its local-interest

street-style niche and onto the desks of the fashion industry's power brokers. Pat McGrath painted makeup in intense, unorthodox ways; Eugene Souleiman dramatized hair; Enninful picked out the powerful pieces and cast edgy, up-and-coming girls—Kate Moss, Naomi Campbell, Devon Aoki, Kristen McMenamy—to turn their forceful faces into Craig McDean's lens. Collectively, they contributed to the rumble of energy that came out of London in the early nineties; the youthful conversion of "low" style into "high" fashion that became an era-defining look.

Enninful brought an innate elegance to the new rawness, a sense of discrimination that developed into a sophisticated point of view. He might have been a club kid who started sourcing clothes from secondhand shops and Portobello Market, but the startling energy and vividness of his styling put him firmly in the fashion vanguard. "It was all Acid House and clubland at the time. I was at clubs like the Mudd Club, watching Leigh Bowery and Boy George. A lot of designers wouldn't lend us clothes, so we'd use things we bought at markets; customize. It was around the time of grunge. There was an urgency and mad creativity. You couldn't distinguish music from fashion, they were so hand-in-hand." Enninful and friends were intent on inventing a new, stripped-down kind of beauty to overthrow the tired glamour of the eighties, but perfecting it brought a fresh set of disciplines. "We were into reality, shooting ratty sweaters and old tweed hipsters. But because it was so minimal, you had to learn to find the one thing that would make your picture."

Born in Ghana, Enninful is one of six children. "My dad was a soldier in the UN Army. We moved to London when I was very young and I was brought up on Ladbroke Grove, with Portobello Market around the corner," he says. "Growing up black in an immigrant family affects how I see the world. The versatility of my work is based on being bombarded by different cultures—living among grunge kids, Rastas, and Indians in Ladbroke Grove, a place that is still the ultimate multicultural mix. For me, at base, it's always about that—a cool girl from Portobello. There was an amazing creative fusion going on there." Enninful attributes his eye for fashion to his mother. "Mum was a seamstress—a fantastic designer, in fact. I learned everything about fashion lingo from her. I remember zipping up her clients; doing up the hooks and eyes, helping her make things. So fashion was a part of me."

Enninful's parents wanted their son to become a lawyer and sent him across the city to be schooled in a "better" neighborhood than that of gritty Notting Hill. His fashion instinct soon stymied that plan when, sitting on a Tube train one day wearing a T-shirt, beat-up Levis, and a pair of cowboy boots, he noticed a man staring at him. "He was Simon Foxton, a stylist for *i-D* magazine; he asked me to model for him." Enninful was sixteen at the time. In 1990 Foxton took the shy, shaven-headed kid to Nick Knight's house in Richmond, where the photographer was shooting a story in which his

assistant, McDean, and Emma Balfour—a waif of the moment—were also modeling. Knight, a founder-photographer at *i-D*, discovered that Enninful wanted to be a stylist and recommended he assist the magazine's fashion director, Beth Summers. When she left her post at *i-D*, Enninful stepped into the job and began broadening the magazine's fashion coverage.

"I thought, 'We have to go to shows'; I wanted *i-D* to be international. So I'd do fashion reports from Paris. I'd commission covers, shopping pages—Terry gave me free reign. It was the best training." The results were soon noticed by Franca Sozzani, editor in chief of Italian *Vogue*, who co-opted him as an occasional freelancer in 1998 to work with McDean and Steven Meisel; the endorsement placed him among the international elite. Before long, designers were not only lending clothes to and advertising in *i-D*, but also tapping Enninful to work on advertising shoots and to style their shows. "I was about twenty-three when Craig landed Calvin Klein—the jeans and khakis advertising for men. Ronnie Cooke Newhouse booked me. We'd never worked outside London; it made me grow up and understand more. When I do editorial, it's about what *I* have to say, but in advertising you have to create a world for someone else. As you get older, you realize it's not just to please yourself. You're not really a stylist until you know that."

Working with Meisel for Italian *Vogue* elevated him to yet another level, "He's like the best teacher in school, who knows your potential and pushes you to achieve it." Enninful styled Meisel's "Young Hollywood" and "Makeover Madness" stories, groundbreaking narratives that dared to push fashion into the realm of socio-documentary but with a satirical subtext. "Young Hollywood" aped tabloid paparazzi reportage with pages of long-lens photos of supposedly off-duty "celebrities" wearing a mishmash of badly styled designer labels; the inept styling was intentional. "Makeover Madness" went even further, using coats, fur, and evening gowns for a story set in a plastic surgery clinic, where the clients do not relinquish their Dolce & Gabbana—even on the operating table.

If this seems a long way from grunge, the thread of Enninful's aesthetic is nonetheless traceable in his ability to tether high-flown fashion to something real and current. Those touches of humor and reality, applied to recognizable fashion situations, are visible in the work he contributes to *Vogue*: evening dresses in a Laundromat, designer bags in diners. As a still-evolving talent this makes him one of the most entertaining stylists to watch today.

Opposite:
Craig McDean
i-D
2002

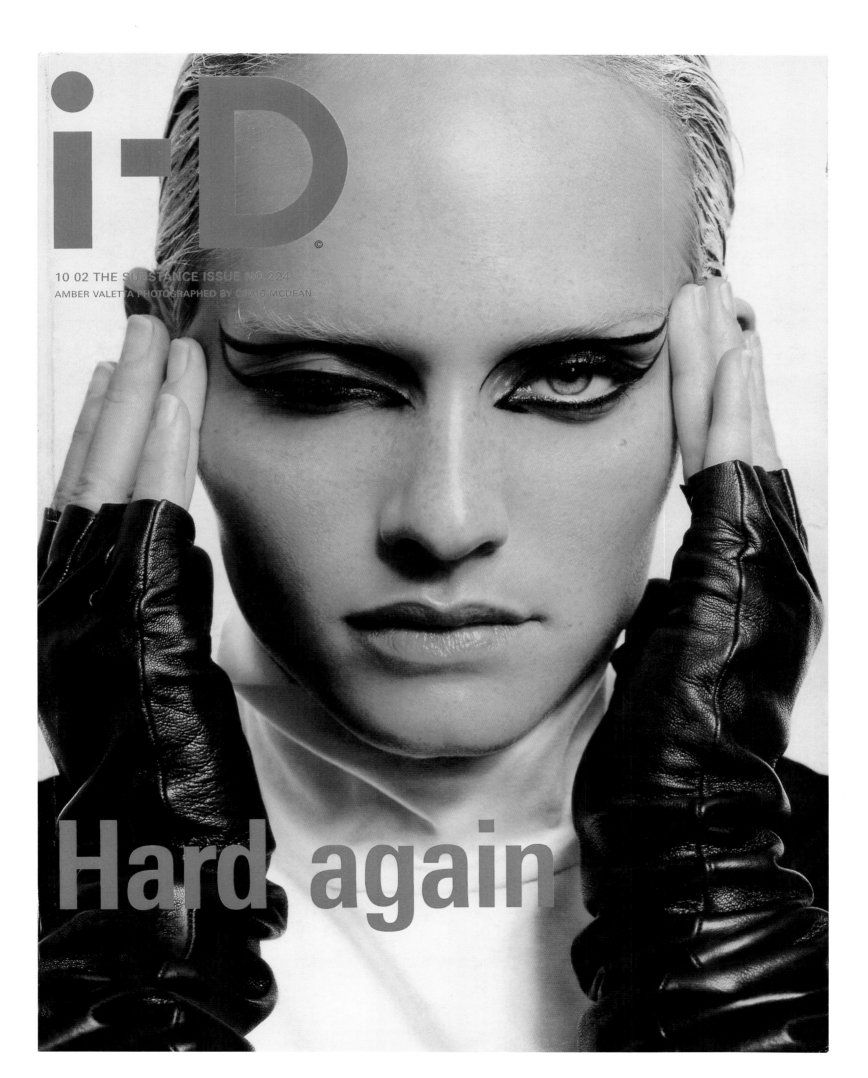

i-D

10 02 THE SUBSTANCE ISSUE NO.224
AMBER VALETTA PHOTOGRAPHED BY CRAIG MCDEAN

Hard again

Opposite:
Steven Meisel
Italian *Vogue*
2005

This page:
Richard Burbridge
Italian *Vogue*
2004

This page:

Top and middle rows:
Alessandro
Dell'Acqua, fall 2006
ready-to-wear.
Photography by
Marcio Madeira/
Style.com

Bottom row: Dolce &
Gabbana, fall 2006
men's ready-to-wear.
Photography by
Marcio Madeira/
Style.com

This page:
Craig McDean
Italian *Vogue*
2003

Overleaf:
Steven Meisel
Italian *Vogue*
2004

EDWARD ENNINFUL

BORN
Ghana (raised in England)

LIVES IN
New York and London

PHOTOGRAPHERS
Craig McDean, Ellen von Unwerth, Emma Summerton, Mario Sorrenti, Mario Testino, Mikael Jansson, Paolo Roversi, Patrick Demarchelier, Richard Burbridge, Steven Klein, Steven Meisel, Tesh

PUBLICATIONS
i-D, Italian Vogue, Japanese Vogue, L'Uomo Vogue, Men's Vogue, V, Vanity Fair, Vogue

CAMPAIGNS
Alessandro Dell'Acqua, Anna Sui, Calvin Klein, Commes Des Garçons, Dolce & Gabbana, Gianfranco Ferré, Giorgio Armani, Hogan, Jil Sander, Lanvin, Missoni, Mulberry, Strenesse, Valentino

Opposite: Edward Enninful, photographed by Tesh for *i-D*, August 1998. This page, top: Enninful as a young boy; middle: the stylist on set; bottom, left: Enninful with his staff, Japanese *Vogue*, October 2003; bottom, right: Enninful photographed by David Slijper for Japanese *Vogue*, October 2003.

CARLYNE CERF DE DUDZEELE

Pages touched by Carlyne Cerf de Dudzeele are so unmistakable there's barely any need to check the credit. If it has vibrant color, piles of jewelry, and laughing girls, it's almost certain to be an image whipped together by her. A force who has traveled at high velocity through French, Italian, and American fashion magazines since the seventies, Cerf de Dudzeele is the embodiment—and, in many ways, the author—of "je ne sais quois"—that seemingly carefree yet discriminating knack for dressing that is quintessentially French.

"It's been with me since I was a child in the south of France, dressing up my cats," she exclaims. "It's about an attitude; how you put on your jewelry, how you carry your bag. I love what people wear in the street, not just the studio. I'm not somebody who follows fashion: I do my own salad."

Cerf de Dudzeele's style is not the chilly chic of Paris, but the breezier, less serious, and far more democratic look that gave *Elle*—a weekly magazine institution in France—its identity at the time of the rise of ready-to-wear. Cerf de Dudzeele was born in Paris and schooled in Saint-Tropez, the then-simple southern fishing port that harbored the one-woman sex and style phenomenon, Brigitte Bardot, in the fifties and sixties. "It's in my bones," Cerf de Dudzeele says. "The more *woman* you can be, the better. A man has to look at a woman and think she is divine. I love strong, sexy, happy women. Grunge killed me; I hate sad clothes, moody makeup. My woman isn't a sad idiot—she's a sexy bitch! That's what I always say: 'Sexy bitch!'."

Cerf de Dudzeele's unique, spontaneous way of working is, she insists, anti-intellectual and unpremeditated. "I cannot work ahead of time, in an office, and decide which accessories will be put with each outfit. I'm not someone who thinks ahead. I change. I might be in another mood tomorrow. My eyes and my gut work with the girl, in the moment. And I show the clothes!" In her view, women couldn't care less about a designer's inspirations or seeing literal top-to-toe repeats of runway looks in magazines. "What they care about is seeing something new to wear!" she states. "I pick from every collection. And I never think I'm doing art—I work on a fashion magazine, and a fashion magazine is for women to look at the pages and be inspired. I'm amazed how many people forget that."

It's quite possible that Cerf de Dudzeele's excessive passion for jewelry can be traced back to her maternal grandmother, Princess Natalia of Montenegro, who was fully acquainted with the art of wearing diamond tiaras and festoons of pearls; though it's not something her granddaughter has particularly analyzed. The middle of three daughters, her enthusiasm for all manner of clothes helped her get her first job as an assistant, through her sister's mother-in-law, Jacqueline Bernardo, editor in chief of French *Marie Claire*. By the seventies she was working at French *Elle*, styling clothes in a mixed-up, cheap-with-expensive manner that anticipated what came to be called "hi-lo" dressing thirty years later. In Cerf de Dudzeele's eyes, a classic Chanel jacket looked best with jeans; captured in the pages of *Elle*, this idea became a standard way of dressing throughout Europe and America in the early eighties. It's a principle she's never dropped, happily throwing on gold Rolexes with Adidas sweatshirts.

In the late eighties and early nineties, periods of tremendous growth for international fashion, Cerf de Dudzeele's talent for maximal, sexy styling won her consultancies with Karl Lagerfeld at Chanel and Gianni Versace. "I was there in the studio when Karl did quilted bags and ballerina pumps in a hundred colors; I still have them all," she declares. With Versace, she styled many of Richard Avedon's high-impact, power advertising campaigns shot on supermodels. "We had so much fun, laughing all night in the studio," she remembers.

A decade spent at American *Vogue* under Anna Wintour was followed by Cerf de Dudzeele's tenure as fashion editor at large at American *Elle*. There, having spent her professional life working with the best photographers—she lists Richard Avedon, Irving Penn, Steven Meisel, Peter Lindbergh, and Patrick Demarchelier—she reached another turning point. "Twenty years ago on a shoot, Patrick Demarchelier said to me I should take my own photographs. I was too paranoid at the time, but then the point came where I said, 'Okay, let's do it.'" Today, stories authored entirely by Carlyne Cerf de Dudzeele—from casting to clothes and pictures—regularly appear in a range of magazines, and she has recently gone freelance so that she can concentrate on photography. "After all," she laughs, "I choose the clothes, the girl, the location. All I wasn't doing was pressing the button. And now it all feels so incredibly easy."

Opposite:
Steven Meisel
Vogue
1989

Opposite:
Steven Meisel
Italian *Vogue*
1990

This page:
Steven Meisel
Vogue
1987

Overleaf:
Steven Meisel
Vogue
1994

Opposite:
Patrick Demarchelier
Vogue
1991

This page:
Peter Lindbergh
Vogue
1988

Pages 242–43:
Peter Lindbergh
Vogue
1988

VOGUE

NOVEMBER $3.00

**the real
cost of
looking
good**

**paris
couture**
*haute but
not haughty*

men
the new bimbos?

fashion

**color
catches on**

INSPIRATION

Carlyne Cerf de Dudzeele drew from tabloid-style images, such as those appearing in *US Weekly*, to create a groundbreaking editorial photographed by Gilles Bensimon for *Elle* in 2003, opposite. Cerf de Dudzeele was the first to bring paparazzi-style shoots to major fashion magazines.

CARLYNE CERF
DE DUDZEELE

BORN

France

LIVES IN

New York

PHOTOGRAPHERS

Gilles Bensimon, Irving Penn, Patrick Demarchelier, Peter
Lindbergh, Richard Avedon, Steven Meisel

CAMPAIGNS

Chanel, Louis Vuitton, Michael Kors, Valentino, Versace

Opposite: Carlyne
Cerf de Dudzeele
photographed by
Mario Testino for
French *Glamour*, 1993.
This page, top: Carlyne
in Venice with friends,
photographed by
Patrick Demarchelier;
middle: two interior
shots of Carlyne's
home: dresser, Michel
Arnaud, *House &
Garden*, 1997; living
room, Roxanne Lowitt,
Chanel magazine, 1993;
bottom: jewelry, Roger-
Viollet, 1993; Princess
Natalia of Montenegro,
Carlyne's grandmother.

PHOTOGRAPHY CREDITS

William Abranowicz © William Abranowicz/Art + Commerce: 217 top left, middle; Mert Alas & Marcus Piggot. Courtesy of Mert Alas & Marcus Piggott: 84, 89, 96, 143; Michel Arnaud © Michel Arnaud: 245 middle; Richard Avedon © 2007 The Richard Avedon Foundation: 4–13; Tina Barney © Tina Barney: 114–15; Fabien Baron © Fabien Baron: 70–71; Cecil Beaton © Cecil Beaton Archive, Sotheby's Picture Library: 27 top right, 34 top left; Gilles Bensimon © Gilles Bensimon: 241; Pete Black © Pete Black: 153, bottom right; Erwin Blumenfeld © Condé Nast: 157, bottom; Richard Burbridge © Richard Burbridge/Art + Commerce: 225; John Chamberlain © John Chamberlain/Artists Rights Society (ARS), New York: 107 bottom; Larry Clark © Larry Clark/courtesy of Luhring Augustine: 174 bottom; Michel Comte. Courtesy of Michel Comte/I-Management: 148; Patrick Demarchelier © Patrick Demarchelier: 106, 238, 245 top; Horst Diekgerdes © Horst Diekgerdes: 179; sin City, Jamie King, 2005 © Dimension Films/Courtesy Everett Collection: 28 bottom; Sin City, Mary Shelton, 2005 Dimension Films/Courtesy Everett Collection: 28 top; Sophie Muller © Sophie Muller: 144, 150–51; Todd Eberle © 2007 by Todd Eberle: 37; Arthur Elgort © Condé Nast: 21, 52; Max Ernst © 2007 Artists Rights Society (ARS), New York/ADAGP, Paris; courtesy Art Resource: 34 bottom right; Photo courtesy Flynet Pictures: 240 bottom; Franz Gertsch © 1978 Franz Gertsch: 107 top; Francois Halard © Francois Halard: 67, fireplace; Edward Hopper © Columbus Museum of Art, Ohio: Museum Purchase, Howald Fund 1954.031: 117 top; Edward Hopper © Fundación Colección Thyssen-Bornemisza, Madrid, Spain. Photography credit Art Resource: 117 bottom; George Hurrell. Courtesy Hurrell Enterprises © George Hurrell: 88; Mikael Jansson © Mikael Jansson/Wilson Wenzel: 72–73, 78–81, 82; Steven Klein © Steven Klein: 20, 62–65, 68; Nick Knight. Photography © Nick Knight, Gemma Ward, Altered States, *W* magazine, 2005: 35; Photography © Nick Knight, Gwen Stefani, *Love. Angel. Music. Baby.* 2004: 140; Photography © Nick Knight, London Loves, *i-D* magazine, 2005: 220; Francis Lawrence © Interscope/Director Francis Lawrence: 142; Dan Lecca © Dan Lecca: 46; Annie Leibovitz © Annie Leibovitz/Contact Press Images: 54–57, 149; 208–09; Sasha Levinson © Sasha Levinson: 153 top, middle, bottom left; Peter Lindbergh © Peter Lindbergh: 83 top, 132–33, 162, 196, 239; © Peter Lindbergh/Estelle Lefebure, Karen Alexander, Rachel Williams, Linda Evangelista, Tatjana Patitz, Christy Turlington, *Vogue* US, Los Angeles, 1990: 242–43; Philip-Lorca diCorcia © Philip-Lorca diCorcia/courtesy the artist and Pace/MacGill Gallery, NY: 116, 118–121; Roxanne Lowit © Roxanne Lowit/Stockland Martel: 245 bottom left; Glen Luchford © Glen Luchford/

Art + Commerce: 90–91; Marcio Madeira © CondéNet: 33, 95, 226; Craig McDean © Craig McDean/Art + Commerce: 58–59, 93, 94, 191, 218, 221, 222–23, 227; Steven Meisel © Steven Meisel/Art + Commerce: 24–26, 29, 60–61, 66, 130–31, 134, 154, 156, 161, 165, 168, 168 top left, 186, 187–88, 199, 210–11, 214–15, 224, 228–29, 232, 234–37; Tom Munro © Tom Munro/CPi: 124; Nickolas Muray © Nickolas Muray Photo Archives: 146 bottom left; Helmut Newton © The Helmut Newton Estate/Maconochie Photography: 2, 16–17; Richard Pandiscio © Richard Pandiscio: 27 bottom; Irving Penn © Condé Nast: 198; Gosta Peterson © Condé Nast: 122 bottom; Diego Rivera. Emmy Lou Packard and Frida Kahlo, 1941; 1 photographic print: b/w, 35 x 31 cm. Courtesy of the Emmy Lou Packard papers, 1900–1901, Archives of American Art, Smithsonian: 146 top; Alberto Rizzo © Condé Nast: 122 top; Franco Rubartelli © Condé Nast: 145, 146 bottom right; John Singer Sargent © Harvard University Art Museums, Fogg Art Museum, Bequest of Grenville L. Winthrop, 1943.316, Photo © David Mathews © President and Fellows of Harvard College: 160 bottom; John Singer Sargent. The Metropolitan Museum of Art, Arthur Hoppock Hearn Fund, 1916 (16.53) Photograph © 1997 The Metropolitan Museum of Art: 160 top; John Scott © John Scott: 185 top left; Davis Sims © David Sims/Art Partner: 74–77; 98; 100–101; 105, 163, 172, David Slijper © David Slijper: 231 bottom right; Mario Sorrenti © Mario Sorrenti/Art Partner: 22; 204–5; Mark Squires © Mark Squires: 147; Joseph Szabo. Cropped from the original photo by Joseph Szabo/courtesy Gitterman Gallery, NY: 174 top, 181; Juergen Teller © Juergen Teller/courtesy Katy Baggott: 30–31, 112, 123, 168, 173, 175–78, 180, 183, 184, 185 middle; Tesh © Tesh: 230; Mario Testino © Mario Testino/Art Partner: 38, 40–45, 47–49, 244; Michael Thompson © Michael Thompson: 158–59; Deborah Turbeville © Condé Nast: 18–19; Ed van der Elsken © Ed van der Elsken/Nederlands Fotomuseum/courtesy Annet Gelink Gallery: 102; Unknown: 14–15, 34 bottom left, 157 top, 197; Inez van Lamsweerde and Vinoodh Matadin © Inez van Lamsweerde and Vinoodh Matadin/Art + Commerce: 36, 50, 86–87, 92, 103, 104, 108–110, 126, 128–29, 135, 138; JB Villareal © CondéNet: 213; Roger Viollet © Roger Viollet: 245 bottom right; Tony Viramontes © Tony Viramontes: 136–37; Nicholas Vreeland © Nicholas Vreeland: 201 middle; Bruce Weber © Bruce Weber/Little Bear: 164, 166–67, 169 top right and bottom, 194–95, 201 bottom right, 206–7; James White © James White: 43; Ben Wilson © Ben Wilson/Insight News & Features: 240 top; Christopher Wool © Christopher Wool/courtesy of artist and Luhring Augustine: 27 top left; Yelena Yemchuk © Yelena Yemchuk/Streeters: 202, 212; Minori Yoshida © Minori Yoshida: 217 top right and bottom.

ACKNOWLEDGMENTS

Special thanks to Anna Wintour; Jamie Pallot, Candy Pratts Price, Dee Salomon, Dirk Standen, and Art Tavee at Style.com; Sarah Mower; Charles Miers at Rizzoli International Publications; Raul Martinez, Principal, CEO and Executive Creative at AR New York; and to all the stylists and photographers who made this book possible.

With thanks and appreciation to the following individuals for their tireless efforts throughout this project: Jennifer Hirshlag, Hamish Anderson, Alison Baenen, Sabina Warren, Steven Torres, Laura Cattano, and Hadley Peterson at Style.com; Julie Di Filippo, Ellen Nidy, Karen Broderick, Tina Henderson, Maria Pia Gramaglia, Kaija Markoe, and Colin Hough Trapp at Rizzoli International Publications; Anthony Petrillose at Empire Editions; Giulia Cappabianca, Account and Production Supervisor, Adam Pellechia, Art Director, and John Finning at AR New York; Jim Moffat, Leslie Sweeney, Anne Kennedy, Stephen Mayes, Jessica Marx, and Wendy Levey at Art + Commerce; Candice Marks, Sarah Dawes, Lucy Lee, and Karl Kolbitz at Art Partner; Brian Hetherington at Baron & Baron Inc.; Marisa Dricsoll at Bryan Bantry Inc.; Chris Donnellan, Leigh Montville, Bryan Starr, Gretchen Fenston, Marianne Brown, Paul Hawryluk, Dawn Lucas, and Rachel Smalley at Condé Nast Publications Inc.; Kiori Okamoto and Reina Nakagawa at Condé Nast Japan; Jennie Sharpe at Condé Nast Syndication UK; Jeffrey Smith and Ronald Pledge at Contact Press Images; Suzanne Speich at Michel Comte; Mary Peng at Corbis; Catherine Walsh and Dennis Keogh at Coty Prestige; Jeff Dymowski at Creative Photographers Inc.; Joan Reidy at Culture and Reality; D and V Management; Didier Fernandez at DNA Model Management; Nicole Berrie at *Elle* Magazine; Mary Fontamillas at Gucci;

Nancy Gillen, Neha Gandhi, and Anna Levak at *Harper's Bazaar*; Jeanette Hurrell at Hurrell Enterprises; Tony Craig at IMG Models Inc.; Janet Borden at Janet Borden Gallery; Akiki Saeki at Jed Root; Sarah Manson at Katy Baggott Ltd.; Nathan Kilcer at Little Bear Inc.; Caroline Burghardt at Luhring Augustine Gallery; Tiggy Maconochie, Tom Giddings, and Helena Vidalic at Maconochie Photography; Margaret Maldonado and Jennifer Lowitz at Margaret Maldonado; Katie Flash at Mario Sorrenti Studio; Nigel Boekee at Michelle Filomeno Agency, Paris; Martijn van den Broek at Nederlands Fotomuseum; Mimi Muray at Nickolas Muray Photo Archives; Kaylie Mountford at NK Image Ltd.; Alexandra Batsford and Lauren Ponzo at Pace/MacGill Gallery; Sean Conway at Pandiscio Co.; Randy Kabat and Jessie Katz at Prada USA; Frank Wong at Quad Graphics; Lisa Kidd at Rebel Waltz; Norma Stevens, Jennifer Congregane, and James Martin at The Richard Avedon Foundation; Vincent LaSpisa and Richard Tang at Sabin, Bermant & Gould LLP; Ingrid Hass at SHOW Studio; Charlie Savile and Kathryn Scahill at Smile Too; Wendy Hurlock Baker, Archives of American Art, Smithsonian Institution; Carmen Zita and Matthew Thompson at Steven Klein Studio; Simon Horobin at Stockland Martel; Beverley Streeter, Pauliina Lehtonen, and Lisa Gralnek at Streeters London & New York; Christian Patterson at Todd Eberle Studios; Tom Gitterman Gallery; Kathy Angstadt at Universal Music; Richard Boehmcke at *Us Weekly*; Caroline Berton, Mathilde Bulteau, Sophie Laffont, and Aurelie Pellissier at French *Vogue*; Jillian Demling at *Vogue*; Kathryn Typaldos at *W* Magazine; Liz Rosenberg at Warner Brothers Reprise Records; Wilson Murphy at Wilson/Wenzel; Siddhartha Shukla and Courtney Calhoun at Yves Saint Laurent.

Five percent of the retail price will benefit the American Red Cross for every *Stylist* book sold from October 23, 2007 through August 31, 2008 with a minimum donation of $15,000.

The American Red Cross name and emblem are used with its permission, which in no way constitutes an endorsement, express or implied, of any product or company.

First published in the United States of America in 2007 by
Rizzoli International Publications, Inc.
300 Park Avenue South
New York, NY 10010
www.rizzoliusa.com

2007 2008 2009 2010 2011 / 10 9 8 7 6 5 4 3 2 1

Printed in China

ISBN-13: 978-0-8478-2924-8

Library of Congress Catalog Control Number: 2007931678